DORLING KINDERSLEY **DK** VISUAL DICTIONARIES

THE VISUAL
DICTIONARY *of the* AMERICAN
CIVIL WAR

Plume

Federal eagle

Chin strap

Leather visor

MILITIA SHAKO

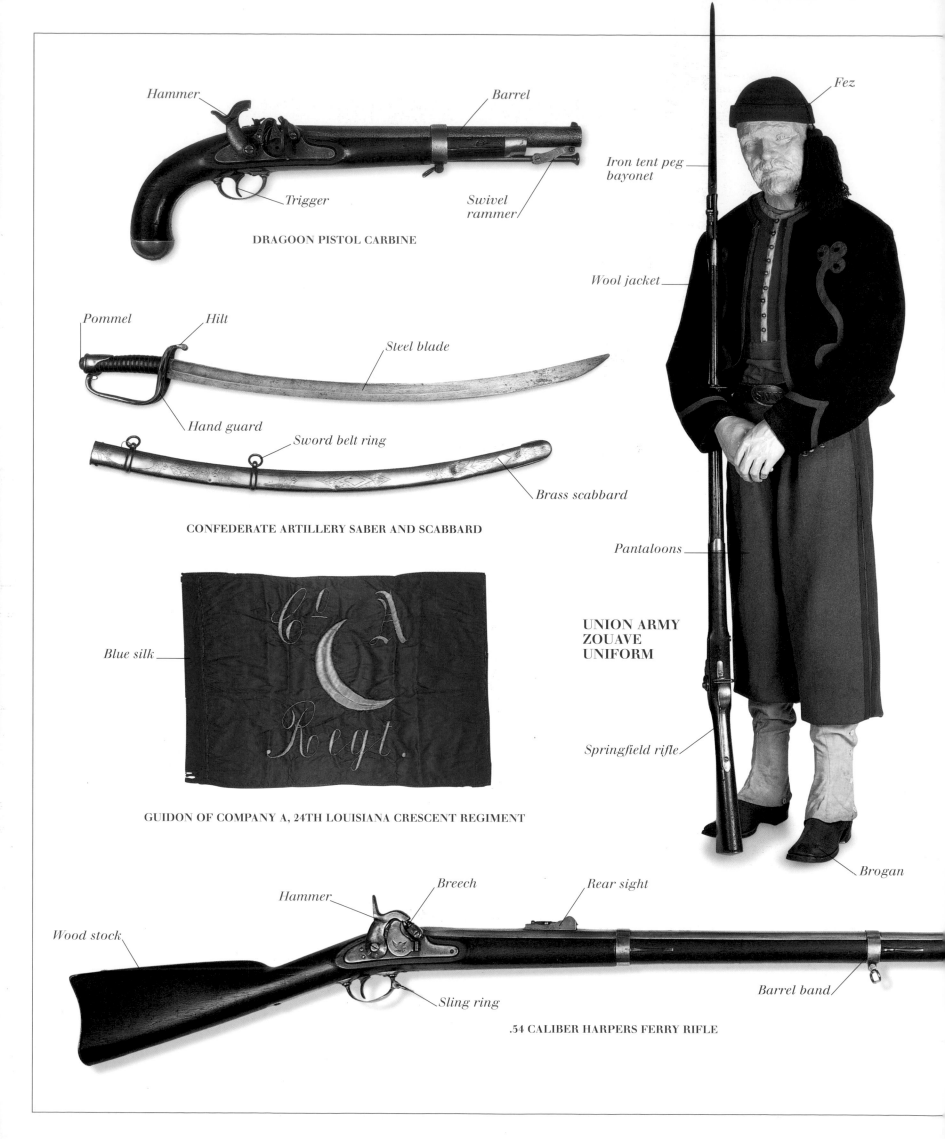

Hammer

Barrel

Trigger

Swivel rammer

DRAGOON PISTOL CARBINE

Fez

Iron tent peg bayonet

Wool jacket

Pommel

Hilt

Steel blade

Hand guard

Sword belt ring

Brass scabbard

CONFEDERATE ARTILLERY SABER AND SCABBARD

Pantaloons

UNION ARMY ZOUAVE UNIFORM

Blue silk

C° A

C

Regt.

Springfield rifle

GUIDON OF COMPANY A, 24TH LOUISIANA CRESCENT REGIMENT

Brogan

Hammer

Breech

Rear sight

Wood stock

Sling ring

Barrel band

.54 CALIBER HARPERS FERRY RIFLE

DORLING KINDERSLEY 📖 VISUAL DICTIONARIES

THE VISUAL
DICTIONARY *of the* AMERICAN
CIVIL WAR

Written by
JOHN STANCHAK

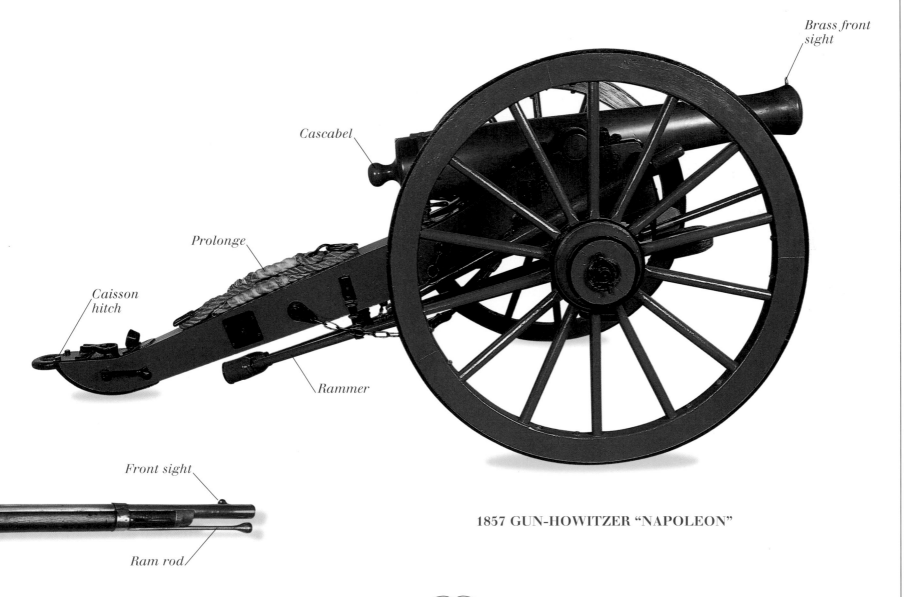

Brass front
sight

Cascabel

Prolonge

*Caisson
hitch*

Rammer

Front sight

Ram rod

1857 GUN-HOWITZER "NAPOLEON"

DORLING KINDERSLEY

DORLING KINDERSLEY

DK www.dk.com

PROJECT EDITOR BETH ADELMAN
ADDITIONAL EDITING CRYSTAL COBLE

DESIGNER TOM CARLING, CARLING DESIGN INC.
PHOTOGRAPHER DAVE KING
COVER DESIGN GUS YOO

PHOTO RESEARCH CRYSTAL COBLE
PRODUCTION SARA GORDON

PUBLISHER SEAN MOORE
EDITORIAL DIRECTOR LAVONNE CARLSON
ART DIRECTOR DIRK KAUFMAN

Hinged leather case

Velvet lining

Ambrotype

Brass frame

A BLACK MEMBER OF
THE 1ST LOUISIANA NATIVE GUARDS

FIRST PUBLISHED IN GREAT BRITAIN IN 2000 BY
DORLING KINDERSLEY LIMITED,
9 HENRIETTA STREET, LONDON WC2E 8PS
2 4 6 8 10 9 7 5 3 1

PUBLISHED IN THE UNITED STATES BY
DK PUBLISHING, INC.
95 MADISON AVENUE
NEW YORK, NEW YORK 10016

COPYRIGHT © 2000 DORLING KINDERSLEY PUBLISHING, INC.
TEXT COPYRIGHT © 2000 JOHN STANCHAK

A CIP catalogue record for this book is
available from the British Library

ISBN 0-7513-1185-5

REPRODUCED BY COLOURSCAN, SINGAPORE
PRINTED AND BOUND BY ARTES GRÁFICAS TOLEDO S.A.U.
D.L. TO: 47 - 2000

Contents

Photo of a soldier

Fob

Brass coins

CONFEDERATE AND HIS PLEDGE

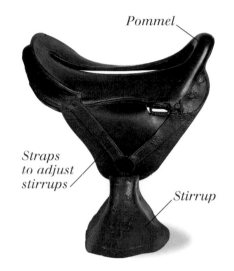

Pommel

Straps to adjust stirrups

Stirrup

CAVALRY SADDLE

Clear center

Amber tinted lens

SHARPSHOOTER'S SPECTACLES

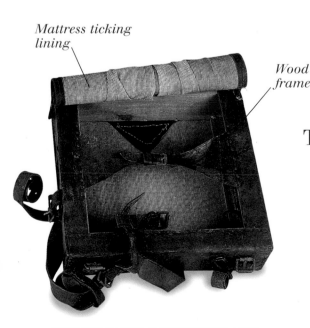

Mattress ticking lining

Wood frame

HOMEMADE CONFEDERATE KNAPSACK

Solid iron shot

Wooden sabot

12-POUND SOLID SHOT

Cockade

Plume

Brass buttons

Gold braid

Swallow tails

UNION NAVY OFFICER'S DRESS JACKET AND CHAPEAU

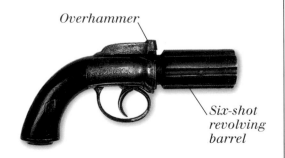

Overhammer

Six-shot revolving barrel

PEPPERBOX PISTOL

Foot soldiers

FROM APRIL 1861 TO APRIL 1865, THREE MILLION men joined the fighting forces of the Union and the Confederacy. Although both sides conscripted soldiers, most were volunteers and the majority served in the infantry. An infantryman, or foot soldier, walked or marched everywhere, carrying equipment, ammunition, personal items, and a field pack – a load that could weigh up to 40 pounds – and a 9- to 10-pound single-shot, muzzle-loading rifle. The Union soldiers' uniforms were made of heavy blue wool. Regulations called for Confederate uniforms to be made of gray wool, but shortages sometimes made that impossible. Much that Civil War soldiers wore and carried was copied from the French military, because in the mid-1800s the French army was considered the world's best. The standard infantry cap, for instance, was the French kepi. Some tactics were also modeled on those Napoleon had used early in that century. The deadliest of these called for a mass of infantrymen to fire one or two rounds with their rifles, then sweep the field with bayonets. But in the Civil War, the power of the troops' heavy-caliber rifles often made bayonet charges unnecessary.

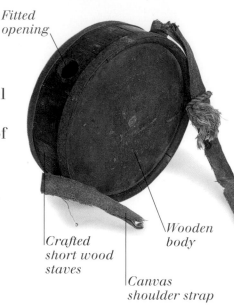

HOMEMADE CONFEDERATE CANTEEN

Fitted opening

Crafted short wood staves

Wooden body

Canvas shoulder strap

RIFLES

Percussion cap was placed here

Hammer

Folding long-range sight

Tempered steel barrel

Walnut stock

Sling ring

Trigger

Steel trigger guard

Brass barrel band

.54 CALIBER HARPERS FERRY RIFLE

Sling loop

Hammer

Folding long-range sight

Barrel

British armory stamp

Sling loop

Trigger

Brass trigger guard

.577 CALIBER BRITISH ENFIELD RIFLE

Butt plate

INFANTRYMAN'S BAYONETS
All Civil War infantrymen carried simple three-sided spike-like bayonets, or the rarer knife-edged sword bayonets, and were expected to use them to take on enemy troops in hand-to-hand combat.

Regulation kepi

Wool uniform coat

Barrel socket

Lug fitting

Edged blade top

Brass hilt

Tempered steel edge

SWORD BAYONET

Barrel socket

Steel blade

Barrel lug fitting

Three-sided spike

SPIKE BAYONET

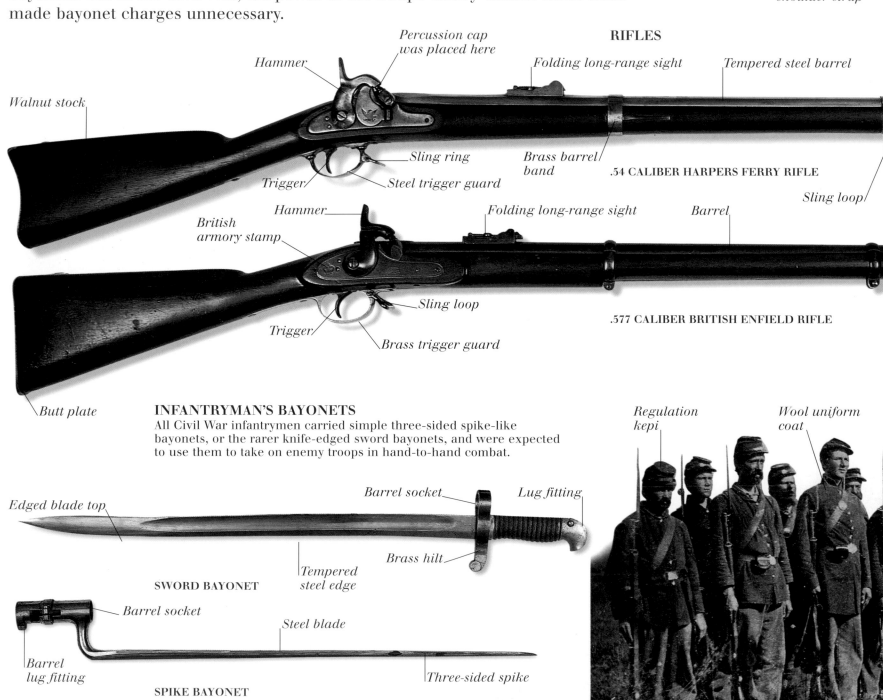

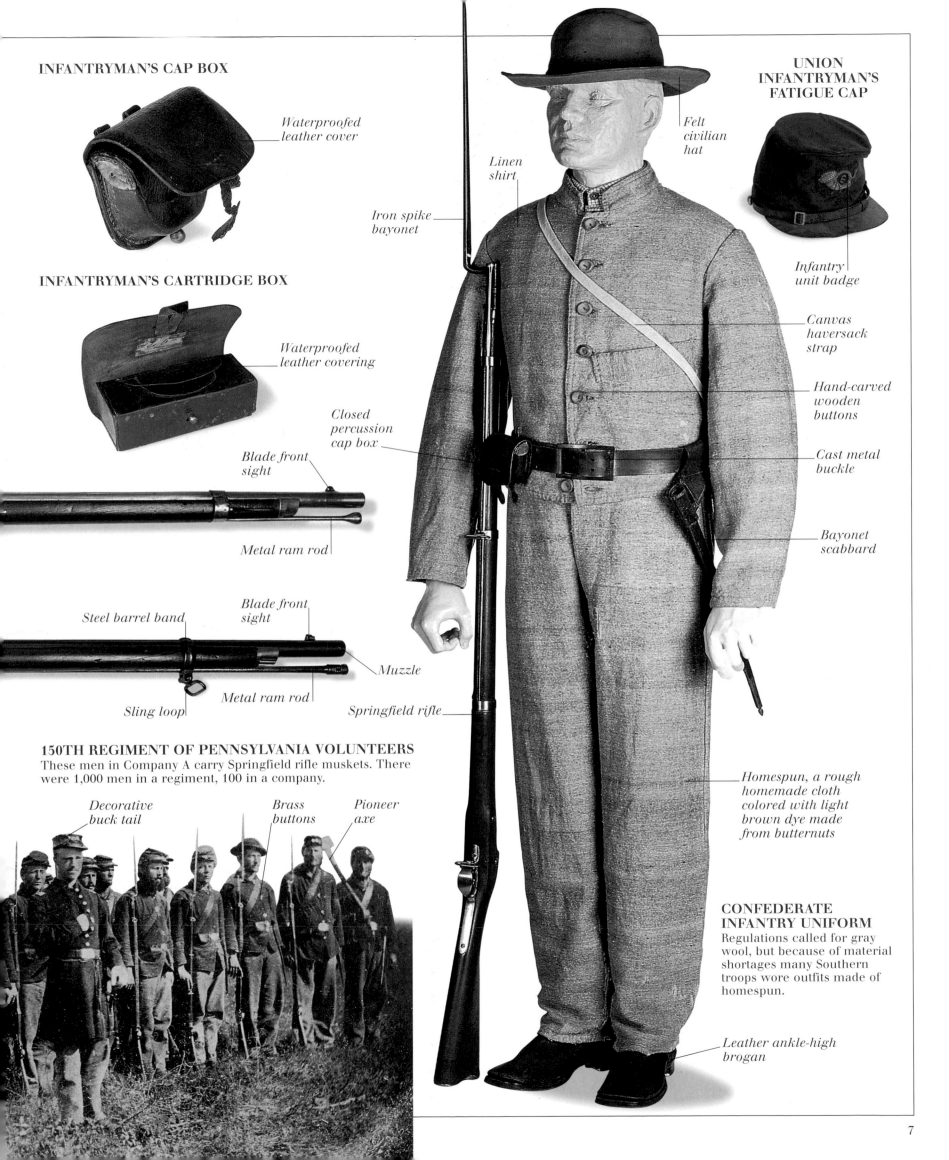

INFANTRYMAN'S CAP BOX

Waterproofed leather cover

INFANTRYMAN'S CARTRIDGE BOX

Waterproofed leather covering

Blade front sight

Metal ram rod

Steel barrel band

Blade front sight

Sling loop

Metal ram rod

Muzzle

150TH REGIMENT OF PENNSYLVANIA VOLUNTEERS
These men in Company A carry Springfield rifle muskets. There were 1,000 men in a regiment, 100 in a company.

Decorative buck tail

Brass buttons

Pioneer axe

UNION INFANTRYMAN'S FATIGUE CAP

Felt civilian hat

Linen shirt

Iron spike bayonet

Infantry unit badge

Canvas haversack strap

Hand-carved wooden buttons

Closed percussion cap box

Cast metal buckle

Bayonet scabbard

Springfield rifle

Homespun, a rough homemade cloth colored with light brown dye made from butternuts

CONFEDERATE INFANTRY UNIFORM
Regulations called for gray wool, but because of material shortages many Southern troops wore outfits made of homespun.

Leather ankle-high brogan

Gunners

THE CANNON WAS the heaviest and deadliest weapon a Civil War soldier had at his disposal. Artillerymen (also called cannoneers or gunners), the men who worked the big guns, were considered specialists and were trained separately. While infantrymen marched, gunners often rode on the draft animals that pulled their big guns, or on the backs of wheeled caissons and ammunition chests. In both the Union and Confederate armies, field artillerymen wore short jackets, knee-length boots, and were identified by the red facings on their jackets and red stripes sewn down the outside seam of their trousers. Because of this, in both armies the nickname for a gunner was "redleg." They also carried a variety of pistols, carbines, short swords, and sabers to defend the cannons from any infantry assault. Artillerymen traveled with a great deal of heavy equipment and ammunition for their guns, as well as their own camp equipment, and equipment and food for their draft horses. Because of this, some claimed they worked twice as hard as any horse soldier and three times as hard as any foot soldier.

UNION OFFICERS POSE WITH A HEAVY ARTILLERY PIECE AND GRAPESHOT

CONFEDERATE OFFICER'S KEPI

Red fabric denotes artillery

Artillery insignia

Leather visor

CAP INSIGNIA

Crossed brass cannons

OFFICER'S JACKET AND GLOVES
The jacket of Confederate Major D.C. Merwin is missing the right sleeve because Merwin was wounded and his right arm had to be amputated. He continued to serve after he recovered.

Red artillery collar facing

Brass button

Wool fabric

Cotton lining

CONFEDERATE ARTILLERY COMPANY FLAG

January 1863 Battle honor

May 1862 battle honor

April 1862 battle honor

WASHINGTON 5th CO. N.O. ARTILLERY

Reinforced canvas border

The Washington Artillery, a New Orleans unit, was a volunteer militia regiment first organized in 1838. They served in all of America's wars through 1945.

September 1862 battle honor

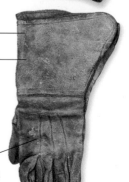

Gauntlet cuff

Two left gloves, given to Merwin by his men

Buffed leather with reinforcing ribs

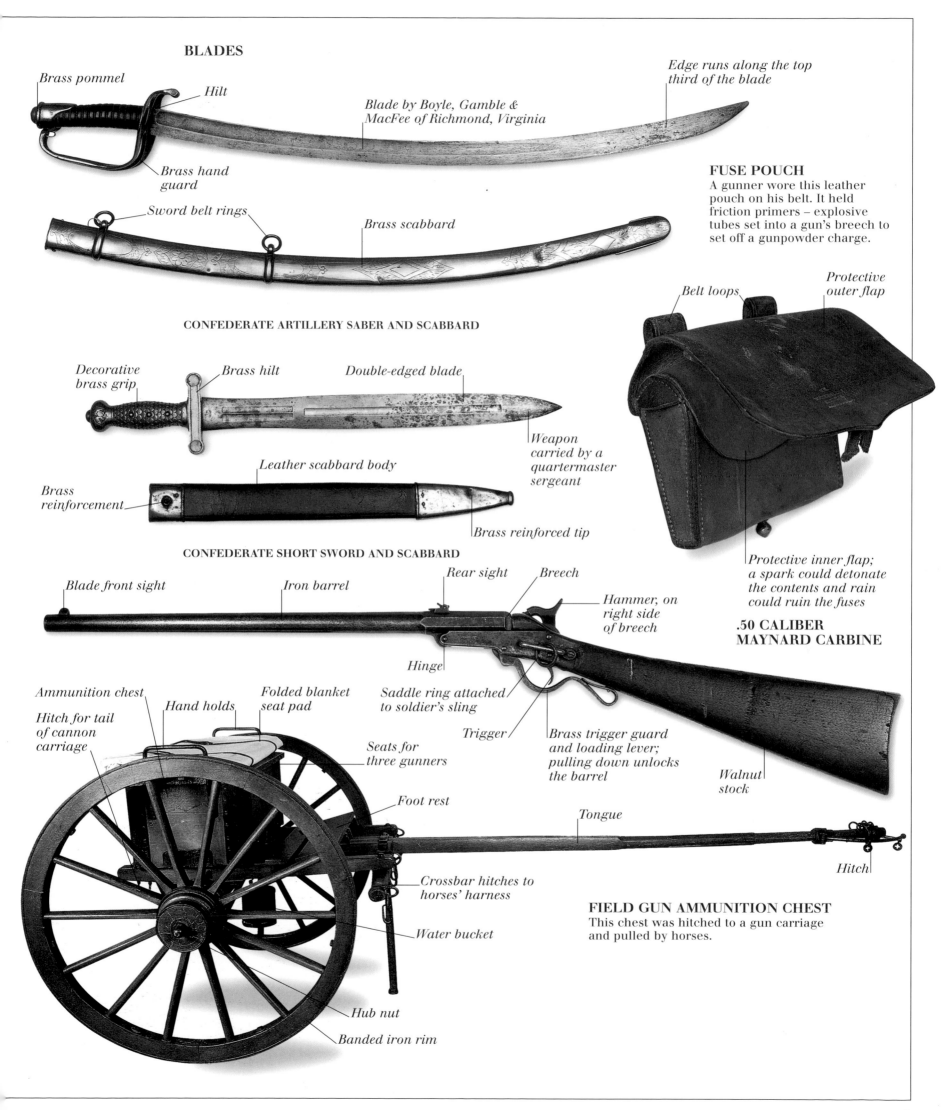

BLADES

Brass pommel

Hilt

Edge runs along the top third of the blade

Blade by Boyle, Gamble & MacFee of Richmond, Virginia

Brass hand guard

Sword belt rings

Brass scabbard

CONFEDERATE ARTILLERY SABER AND SCABBARD

Decorative brass grip

Brass hilt

Double-edged blade

Weapon carried by a quartermaster sergeant

Leather scabbard body

Brass reinforcement

Brass reinforced tip

CONFEDERATE SHORT SWORD AND SCABBARD

FUSE POUCH
A gunner wore this leather pouch on his belt. It held friction primers – explosive tubes set into a gun's breech to set off a gunpowder charge.

Protective outer flap

Belt loops

Protective inner flap; a spark could detonate the contents and rain could ruin the fuses

.50 CALIBER MAYNARD CARBINE

Blade front sight

Iron barrel

Rear sight

Breech

Hammer, on right side of breech

Hinge

Saddle ring attached to soldier's sling

Trigger

Brass trigger guard and loading lever; pulling down unlocks the barrel

Walnut stock

Ammunition chest

Hand holds

Folded blanket seat pad

Hitch for tail of cannon carriage

Seats for three gunners

Foot rest

Tongue

Hitch

Crossbar hitches to horses' harness

FIELD GUN AMMUNITION CHEST
This chest was hitched to a gun carriage and pulled by horses.

Water bucket

Hub nut

Banded iron rim

Horse soldiers

In both the Union and Confederate armies, cavalry service was considered the most glamorous. Generals assigned mounted troops to scouting duty and expected them to cover the withdrawal of an army or to pursue retreating enemy soldiers. To carry out these missions, horse soldiers were fitted out with a wide variety of firearms. In the early days of the war, a number of Confederate mounted units, striving for a 17th century cavalier look, wore wide-brimmed, plumed hats. But cavalrymen – direct military descendants of medieval knights – were best known for carrying heavy, curved sabers. A trooper outfitted for action traveled light, carrying his pistol, carbine, saber, ammunition, canteen, a blanket roll, some personal things, and a few light horse care items in his saddle bags. If he was involved in a long campaign, his unit's camp equipment, horse shoeing tools, fodder, and veterinary items were packed in wagons that followed along the line of march.

HAND GUNS

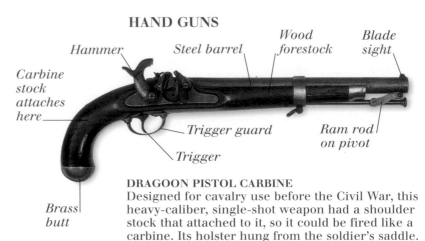

Hammer · Steel barrel · Wood forestock · Blade sight
Carbine stock attaches here · Trigger guard · Ram rod on pivot · Trigger · Brass butt

DRAGOON PISTOL CARBINE
Designed for cavalry use before the Civil War, this heavy-caliber, single-shot weapon had a shoulder stock that attached to it, so it could be fired like a carbine. Its holster hung from the soldier's saddle.

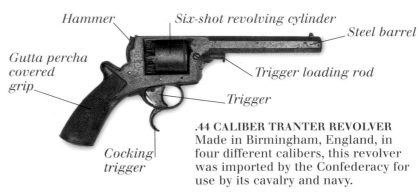

Hammer · Six-shot revolving cylinder · Steel barrel
Gutta percha covered grip · Trigger loading rod · Trigger · Cocking trigger

.44 CALIBER TRANTER REVOLVER
Made in Birmingham, England, in four different calibers, this revolver was imported by the Confederacy for use by its cavalry and navy.

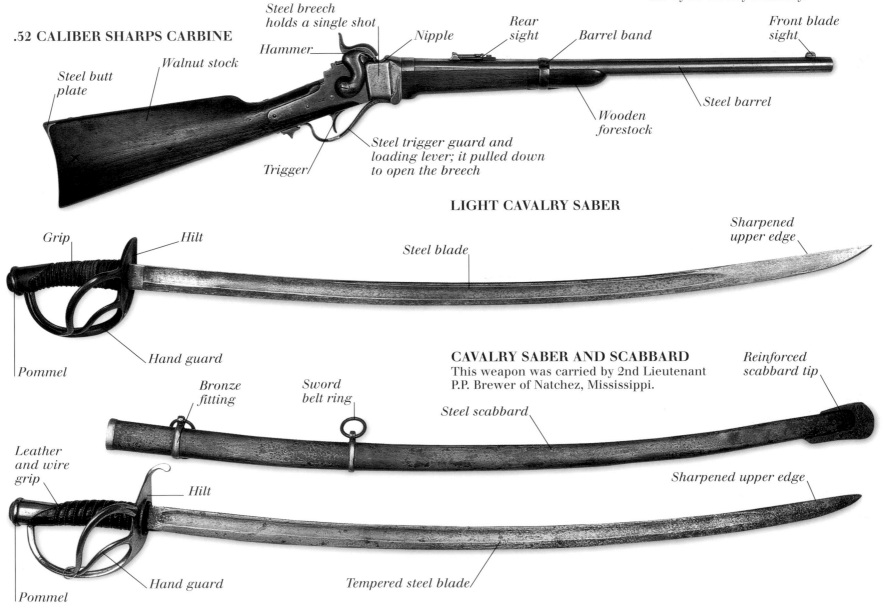

.52 CALIBER SHARPS CARBINE

Steel breech holds a single shot · Nipple · Rear sight · Barrel band · Front blade sight
Hammer · Walnut stock · Steel butt plate · Trigger · Steel trigger guard and loading lever; it pulled down to open the breech · Wooden forestock · Steel barrel

LIGHT CAVALRY SABER

Grip · Hilt · Steel blade · Sharpened upper edge
Pommel · Hand guard

CAVALRY SABER AND SCABBARD
This weapon was carried by 2nd Lieutenant P.P. Brewer of Natchez, Mississippi.

Bronze fitting · Sword belt ring · Steel scabbard · Reinforced scabbard tip
Leather and wire grip · Hilt · Sharpened upper edge · Pommel · Hand guard · Tempered steel blade

Chin strap

Kepi

Yellow collar
and jacket
piping signified
cavalry

Decorative
gold braid

Stiff, upright
collar

Brass
button

Cavalry gauntlet

Worsted
wool
trousers

Ankle-high
brogan

**UNION
CAVALRY
UNIFORM**
The short jackets
with yellow facings
enabled horse
soldiers to be
identified at a
distance.

Confederate
battle flag

Plumed
cavalry hat

Leather
carbine
sling

MEN OF THE FIRST VIRGINIA CAVALRY
This sketch of horse soldiers in the field was made
by a British newspaper correspondent.

SADDLE BAG

Buckle to
attache bag
behind saddle
seat

Leather flap

Securing
strap

Split seat

Pommel

CAVALRY SADDLE
This saddle was used by
Confederate Captain
E.M. Hudson. It is made
on the McClellan
pattern, a design created
before the war by future
Union General George
B. McClellan.

Cup
stirrup

Protective flap kept
brush and burrs from
tearing pants

Boot
strap

Built-up sole

**CONFEDERATE
CAVALRY BOOTS**
Taken from the body of Private
Alexander Dimitry, who was killed
in action. Dimitry was a member of
Mosby's Rangers, operating in Blue
Ridge, Virginia.

SPURS
Western-style spurs worn by
Confederate Captain E.M. Hudson.

Security
chain

Rowl

Bronze
heel

Weights flipped
against horse's flanks
and kept him moving

Sailors

MOST CIVIL WAR OFFICERS of the Union and Confederate navies were veterans of U.S. service at sea, as were many Union enlisted men. But many common sailors aboard some of the Confederacy's best-known fighting ships were not Southerners at all. The bulk of the crews on the Confederate commerce raiders on the high seas were foreign-born seamen recruited in European ports, who served for pay and bounty. And many crewmen on Confederate coastal and river vessels were skilled Southern civilians, slaves, laborers, and army soldiers pressed into naval service. Licensed civilian steamboat pilots and experienced ferrymen were also employed by both sides. In this conflict, waged on rivers and bayous as well as at sea, steam-driven armored vessels often took on sail-powered wooden ships, and men with mechanical, iron-working or river navigation skills were as valuable as men who were at ease working high up in a ship's rigging. Formally, both Union and Confederate sailors adopted the same regulations and traditions of the pre-war U.S. navy, even down to the cut of their wool uniforms.

Naval officer

Hawser rope to secure the gun during combat

Spittoon and ashtray

UNION NAVY "POWDER MONKEY"
It was an old naval tradition to accept boys into service. A "powder monkey" was a boy who helped keep gunners supplied with gunpowder and ammunition. All sailors were expected to have some training in working a cannon.

SAILOR'S PISTOL BELT

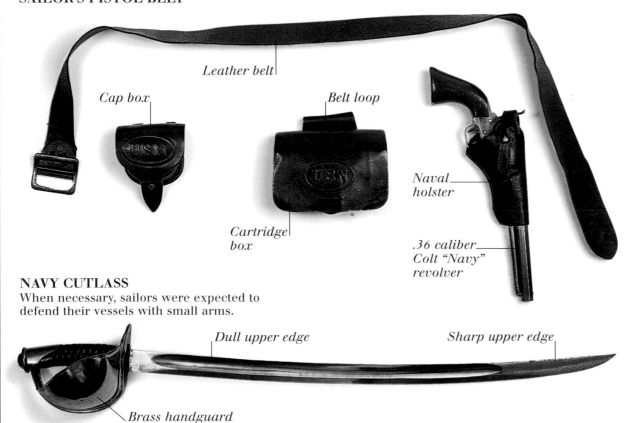

Leather belt

Cap box

Belt loop

Cartridge box

Naval holster

.36 caliber Colt "Navy" revolver

NAVY CUTLASS
When necessary, sailors were expected to defend their vessels with small arms.

Dull upper edge

Sharp upper edge

Brass handguard

HAILING TRUMPET

Mouthpiece

Brass bell

- *Furled sail*
- *Dahlgren gun*
- *Chimney for cook's stove*
- *Ship's wheel*
- *Capstan for raising the ship's anchor*
- *Marine*

PENNANT OF CONFEDERATE NAVY VESSEL C.S.S. MCRAE

Stars represent each Confederate state

UNION OFFICER'S DRESS CHAPEAU

- *Cockade*
- *Plume, damaged by age*
- *Brass button*

UNION OFFICER'S DRESS JACKET

- *Upright collar*
- *Brass buttons*
- *Napoleonic design*
- *Sleeve braid indicates rank*
- *Swallow tails*

ABOARD A UNION NAVAL VESSEL

The Union navy, unlike the Union army, was racially integrated. Cramped ship-board conditions and heavy duty requirements did not allow for separate work and living accommodations for black and white seamen.

C.S.S. ALABAMA

Captained by Raphael Semmes, this Confederate commerce raider roamed the globe sinking Union merchant ships. It was finally sunk in 1864 by the U.S.S. Kearsarge off Cherbourg, France.

Elite units

CIVIL WAR ARMIES WERE LARGELY made up of volunteer units raised by wealthy community leaders. If the man who raised the company or regiment had a special military interest, he often outfitted his men in custom uniforms, had them perform specific drills or train in special skills. Some popular elite units were artillery gunners, cavalry scouts, sharpshooters, lancers, and troops fitted out in the unusual uniforms of French Algerian soldiers, the Zouaves. Union Colonel Hiram Berdan's U.S. Regiments of Sharpshooters and Confederate Colonel Roberdeau Wheat's Zouaves, the Louisiana Tiger Rifles, are two interesting examples. Wheat was a Louisiana attorney with a taste for military adventure. When the Civil War broke out, he raised a unit of toughs from the New Orleans waterfront – the 1st Louisiana Special Battalion – fitted them out in Zouave uniforms and taught them the quick-stepping drills of the French Zouaves. Berdan's sharpshooters were fitted out with green caps and uniforms and given .52 caliber Sharps rifles. Berdan's two regiments were eventually broken up into small units and assigned throughout the Union's Army of the Potomac. Serving as snipers and skirmishers, they could disable entire artillery batteries with their accurate fire from concealed positions.

UNIFORM JACKET OF RUSH'S LANCERS

Jacket of Lancer Charles Masland

Brass buttons

Blue wool, discolored by age

Nine-foot shaft

LANCE CARRIED BY RUSH'S 6TH PENNSYLVANIA CAVALRY
The men of the Lancers were recruited from Philadelphia High Society by Colonel Richard Rush. Their dashing lances proved inefficient in wooded country, however, and in 1863 they exchanged them for carbines.

ZOUAVE REGIMENT
Officers and enlisted men of a Zouave regiment from New York State. These uniforms, and the Zouave's world-famous fancy, quick-stepping drills, were adopted by proud volunteer regiments in both the North and South.

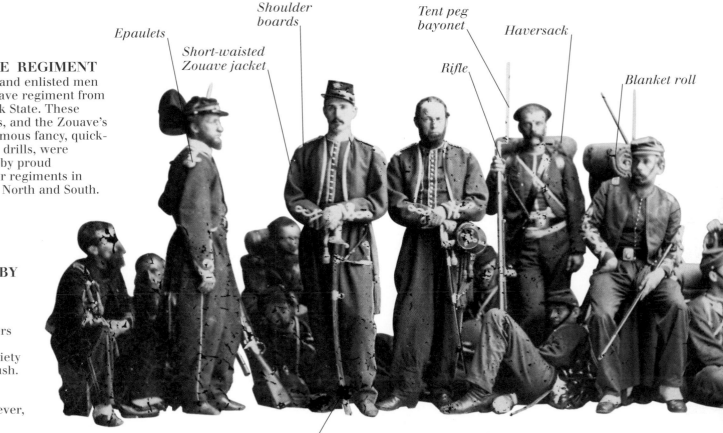

Epaulets

Shoulder boards

Short-waisted Zouave jacket

Tent peg bayonet

Rifle

Haversack

Blanket roll

Infantry officer's combat sword

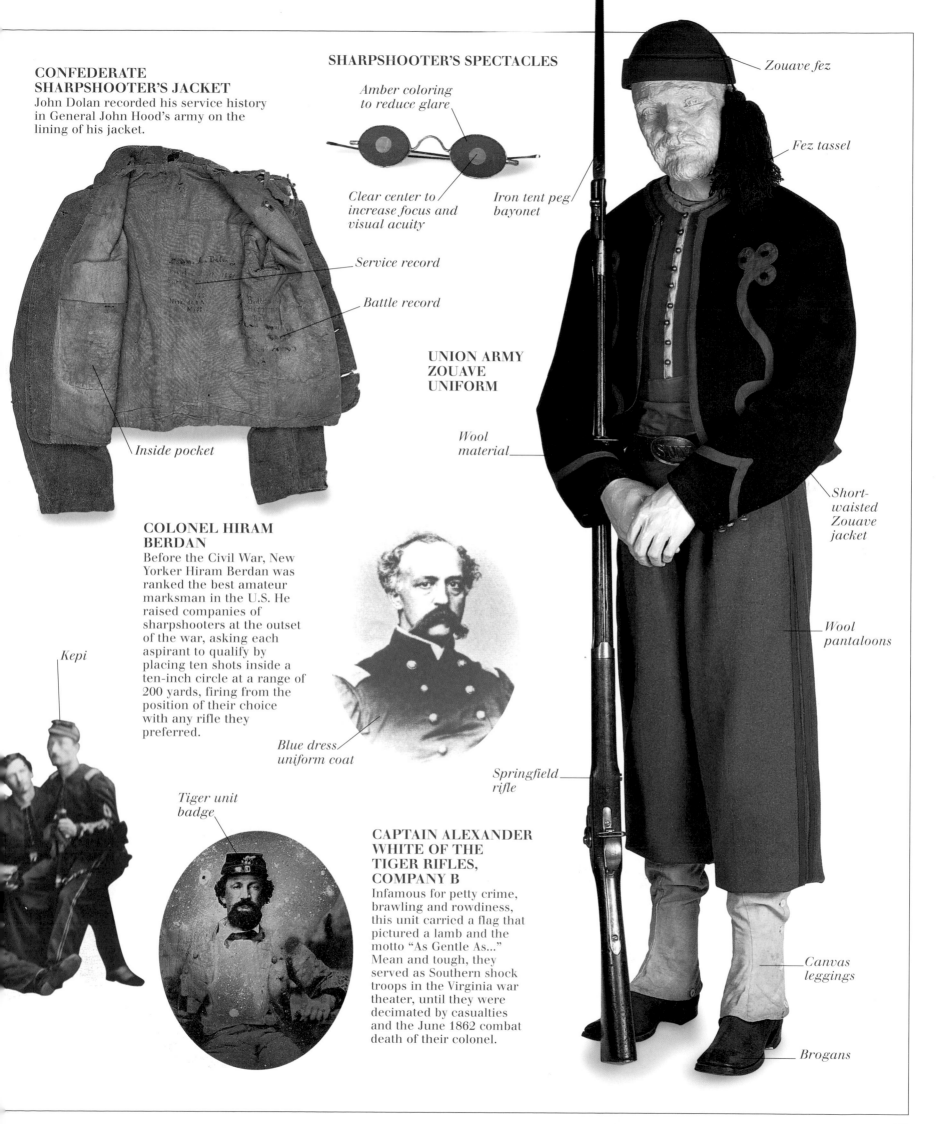

CONFEDERATE SHARPSHOOTER'S JACKET
John Dolan recorded his service history in General John Hood's army on the lining of his jacket.

Inside pocket

SHARPSHOOTER'S SPECTACLES

Amber coloring to reduce glare

Clear center to increase focus and visual acuity

Service record

Battle record

Iron tent peg bayonet

Zouave fez

Fez tassel

UNION ARMY ZOUAVE UNIFORM

Wool material

Short-waisted Zouave jacket

COLONEL HIRAM BERDAN
Before the Civil War, New Yorker Hiram Berdan was ranked the best amateur marksman in the U.S. He raised companies of sharpshooters at the outset of the war, asking each aspirant to qualify by placing ten shots inside a ten-inch circle at a range of 200 yards, firing from the position of their choice with any rifle they preferred.

Blue dress uniform coat

Kepi

Wool pantaloons

Tiger unit badge

Springfield rifle

CAPTAIN ALEXANDER WHITE OF THE TIGER RIFLES, COMPANY B
Infamous for petty crime, brawling and rowdiness, this unit carried a flag that pictured a lamb and the motto "As Gentle As..." Mean and tough, they served as Southern shock troops in the Virginia war theater, until they were decimated by casualties and the June 1862 combat death of their colonel.

Canvas leggings

Brogans

Black troops

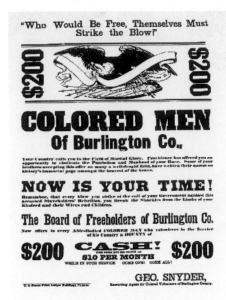

BURLINGTON, VERMONT, RECRUITING POSTER

MORE THAN 175,000 African-American men served in the Union's armed forces, most in the army as members of U.S.C.T. regiments – United States Colored Troops. At the outset of the war, the law forbade blacks from joining the U.S. army. In 1862, Union Major General Benjamin Butler tried to organize army units of black volunteers in New Orleans, but Federal officials declared his units illegal. The U.S. Congress finally approved the organization of black units in July 1862, and the first U.S.C.T. units were formed the following year. U.S.C.T. enlisted men were paid $2 less per month than white volunteers, and were generally treated badly by them. Despite that, several U.S.C.T. units quickly distinguished themselves. One that won fame through tragic and brave combat was the 54th Massachusetts, of Boston. The unit was decimated in an 1863 assault on Confederate-held Fort Wagner outside Charleston, South Carolina. In the South, slaves from plantations located near the fighting often sought refuge behind Northern lines. Union army administrators had no plan to deal with these refugees, and until President Abraham Lincoln issued the Emancipation Proclamation on January 1, 1863, they were legally obliged to return them to their masters.

All U.S.C.T. regiments were led by white officers.

Modern rifle; in reality, many black soldiers were armed with old rifle muskets

CANTEEN

This canteen belonged to Native Guards Lieutenant A. Montieau. New Orleans had a sizeable free black population and a tradition of black military service. But Confederate authorities were not as open-minded, and the regiment was never accepted into the Confederate military.

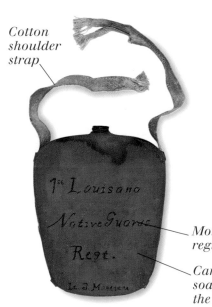

Cotton shoulder strap

Montieau wrote his regiment and name

Canvas cover; soaking it keeps the canteen cool

Cut velvet lining

Brass hinge

Ambrotype image

A BLACK MEMBER OF THE 1ST LOUISIANA NATIVE GUARDS
In the last days of the Civil War, the Confederate Congress, desperate for fighting men, authorized the raising of black units. Defeat came before any could be organized.

FLAG OF THE U.S.C.T. 2ND MASSACHUSETTS CAVALRY

Gold fringe

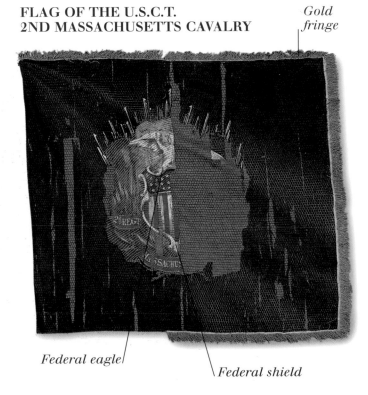

Federal eagle

Federal shield

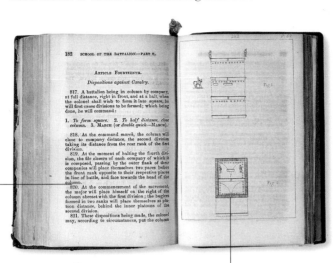

MANUAL USED TO TRAIN NEW RECRUITS
Many former slaves who joined the Union army had been prohibited from learning to read and write. They memorized drills, tactics, and regulations after officers read aloud to them from training manuals.

Kepi

New winter uniform with cape

Text explaining how to fight against cavalry units

Troop deployment diagram

"COME AND JOIN US, BROTHERS"
This lithograph, used to recruit men into the U.S.C.T., is modeled on a photograph of an actual regiment.

Regimental drummer boy

HALF-BROTHERS AND CONFEDERATE VOLUNTEERS
These New Orleans volunteers were half-brothers – one white, one black. They were accepted in southern Louisiana culture but not elsewhere in the Confederacy.

Hand tinting

Brass frame

Coal bucket

City Point, Virginia, wharf

Union supply ships

Supply building

Dish pan

Contrabands wore castoff Union army clothes

CONTRABANDS BUILDING A UNION SUPPLY FACILITY
In 1861 Union Major General Benjamin Butler avoided returning escaped slaves by declaring them the "contraband of war." The army employed many of them as laborers, and soldiers called them "contrabands."

Southern leaders

BETWEEN DECEMBER 1860 AND MAY 1861, when the Southern states seceded from the Union, the government and military of the United States were fractured. Congressmen and senators from states that had seceded abandoned their legislative seats and went home to help form a new government. Some Federal judges from the South resigned their positions rather than support a government they had lost faith in. Army officers and navy commanders wrestled with these same decisions, and many from the South resigned their commissions and went home to organize the defense of the Confederacy. General Joseph E. Johnston and Colonels Robert E. Lee, Albert Sidney Johnston, and P.G.T. Beauregard – all skilled military engineers or veterans of the Mexican War – accepted Confederate generals' commissions and orchestrated the seizure of Fort Sumter in April 1861, victory at the Battle of Bull Run in July 1861, and the creation of the Confederate War Department.

JEFFERSON DAVIS, PRESIDENT OF THE CONFEDERATE STATES OF AMERICA
Davis was a West Point graduate, a Mexican War colonel, a former U.S. Secretary of War, and a Senator from Mississippi. He was supported politically by experienced men like ex-U.S. President John Tyler, a Southerner who took a seat in the Confederate Congress.

Detachable starched collar

Bow tie

GENERAL ROBERT E. LEE
Lee was already famous as the officer who captured militant abolitionist John Brown in 1859. He was offered command of the Union's field army in the East, but declined. When Virginia seceded, Lee resigned from the U.S. army and offered his services to the Confederacy. He served as Jefferson Davis' chief military advisor until taking a field command in May 1862. Today, Arlington National Cemetery is located on the site of Lee's Virginia home.

Rank insignia

Cavalry saber

A colonel wore three stars, while a general wore three stars inside a wreath; Lee never adopted the full insignia of his rank

LIEUTENANT GENERAL NATHAN BEDFORD FORREST
Forrest became a millionaire by trading in slaves and real estate. He earned a reputation as a brilliant tactician and a fierce cavalry officer. After the war, Forrest helped found the Ku Klux Klan.

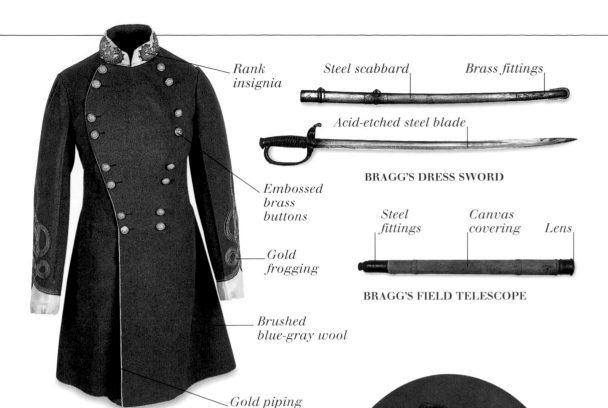

Rank insignia

Steel scabbard   Brass fittings

Acid-etched steel blade

BRAGG'S DRESS SWORD

Embossed brass buttons

Steel fittings   Canvas covering   Lens

Gold frogging

BRAGG'S FIELD TELESCOPE

Brushed blue-gray wool

Gold piping

BRAGG'S DRESS UNIFORM COAT

GENERAL BRAXTON BRAGG

Bragg commanded the Confederate army at Chickamauga and Chattanooga, and was one of Jefferson Davis' highest-ranking generals. He was also one of the most contentious. His feud with Lieutenant General James Longstreet and other subordinates during the 1863 siege of Chattanooga required Davis' intervention.

Initials "CS" for Confederate States   Dress sword

LIEUTENANT GENERAL "STONEWALL" JACKSON

Thomas Jonathan Jackson was a poor boy from Virginia who won an appointment to West Point and served in the U.S. army during the Mexican War. When Virginia seceded, he was an obscure professor at the Virginia Military Institute. In the Confederate army he rose to lieutenant general and corps commander. Jackson helped deliver Confederate victories at the Second Battle of Bull Run and at Chancellorsville. He died of wounds received at Chancellorsville in May 1863.

Jackson's dress uniform

MAJOR GENERAL J.E.B. STUART

Stuart was a dashing Virginia cavalry officer, well known for his flashy personal style. He and many of his troops wore plumed cavalier-style hats and sang on long rides, while Stuart's aide, Joe Sweeny, played the banjo. Stuart died in 1864 of wounds received during the Battle of Yellow Tavern.

Early in the war, Beauregard wore his old U.S. engineers uniform

GENERAL PIERRE GUSTAVE TUTANT BEAUREGARD

Beauregard was the South's first hero general. He commanded the forces that bombarded Fort Sumter in April 1861, the act that opened the Civil War. He also had command of large numbers of forces at the First Battle of Bull Run in July 1861 and the Battle of Shiloh in April 1862. After the war he retired to New Orleans, where he reigned as a local celebrity.

Brass fittings   Fabric straps

Tooled leather straps   Brass rowls   Cavalry jacket

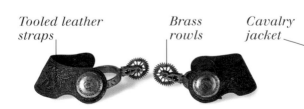

BEAUREGARD'S SPURS
These Western-style spurs were made for U.S. General Persifor Smith, who wore them during the Mexican War. Smith's son, a Confederate officer, gave them to Beauregard in 1862.

BEAUREGARD'S EPAULETS

Northern leaders

THE DEFECTION TO THE SOUTH of so many skilled military professionals set back the Union cause at the outset of the war. But the names of some who stood by the Union surprised the public. General-in-Chief of the U.S. Army Winfield Scott, an elderly Virginian, formed the first plan to subdue the rebellious states. George Henry Thomas, also a Virginian, retained his U.S. army commission, earned the rank of major general and won battlefield distinction at Chickamauga and Nashville. Major Robert Anderson, a Kentuckian and a member of a slave-holding family, was the officer who held Fort Sumter in the face of Confederate cannon. Newly commissioned generals and colonels George B. McClellan, Ambrose Burnside, Joseph Hooker, George G. Meade, William T. Sherman, and Ulysses S. Grant were all relative unknowns. They sometimes failed on the battlefield and were frequently forced to reorganize their armies. Their commander-in-chief, Abraham Lincoln, had no military experience. That this group, in the end, bested the talented and experienced Confederate leadership is not only a credit to the industrial might of the North and Lincoln's moral vision, but to these officer's' persistence, innovation, and will.

Background represents western Virginia, which he helped subdue early in the war

Kerchief

Officer's sash

Dress sword

Bow tie

Watch chain

Eyeglasses

ABRAHAM LINCOLN, PRESIDENT OF THE UNITED STATES OF AMERICA

Lincoln, the commander-in-chief, was a former general practice attorney from Illinois. After serving one term in Congress (during which he opposed American involvement in the Mexican War), he made a living representing railroads in legal actions. Lincoln was the Republican Party's first successful Presidential candidate. When he took office, he had no long-term connections or friendships inside the Washington establishment or the U.S. military.

LIEUTENANT GENERAL ULYSSES S. GRANT AND HIS STAFF

Lieutenant Colonel Eli Parker, Grant's military secretary and the man who wrote up the surrender terms for Robert E. Lee. Parker was a Native American and an officer of the Seneca tribe in New York. He was Commissioner of Indian Affairs during Grant's presidency.

General Grant

Major General John Rawlings, later Secretary of War during Grant's presidency

Brigadier General Frederick Dent, Grant's brother-in-law

Background represents Georgia, which he subdued in 1864

Bedroll

Sherman's war horse "Lexington"

MAJOR GENERAL WILLIAM T. SHERMAN

A West Point graduate, Sherman served in California before resigning his commission to try careers in business and education. He left a teaching position in Louisiana to join the Union army. Serving under Grant, he fought at Shiloh, Vicksburg, and Chattanooga. He is best known for leading the army that took Atlanta and marched to the sea.

SHERMAN'S CAMPAIGN HAT

The general wore this hat through battles and marches from Chattanooga, Tennessee, to Savannah, Georgia. A Union businessman arriving with supplies at Savannah was stunned by Sherman's "shocking bad hat," and swapped him a new one for this war-worn souvenir.

Gold satin trim

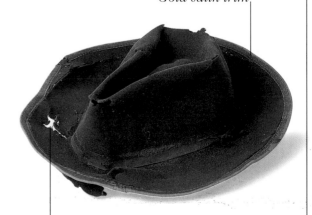

Holes and damage caused by hard wear, not shot or shell

Hand guns

THE SHOOTING STARTED ON APRIL 12, 1861, before dawn. Confederate troops in Charleston, South Carolina, firing at Fort Sumter were armed with weapons seized from U.S. arsenals or with U.S. weapons provided by militia organizations. For more than three months, Southerners from Texas to Georgia had been gathering up government ordinance, ensuring that when war came both armies would go into combat carrying the same variety of pistols, blades, and rifles. Many Union troops and even more Confederates went off to war carrying personal arms as well: heavy-caliber hunting rifles, squirrel guns, shotguns, pocket revolvers, out-sized knives made by village blacksmiths, and even brass knuckles. A big assortment of these items were gathered up from battlefields after the war's first engagements. But as time went by troops came to rely on the sturdy standard weapons their armies supplied. The most common pistols were revolvers made by Colt or Remington. They came in .44 caliber "Army" and .36 caliber "Navy" models.

.44 CALIBER COLT "ARMY" REVOLVER, HOLSTERED

.36 CALIBER ARSENAL GANG MOLD

Mold produces nine lead pistol slugs at one time

POCKET PISTOLS

Small hand guns such as these were called "pocket pistols." Many enlisted men carried them on the battlefield in case of emergency.

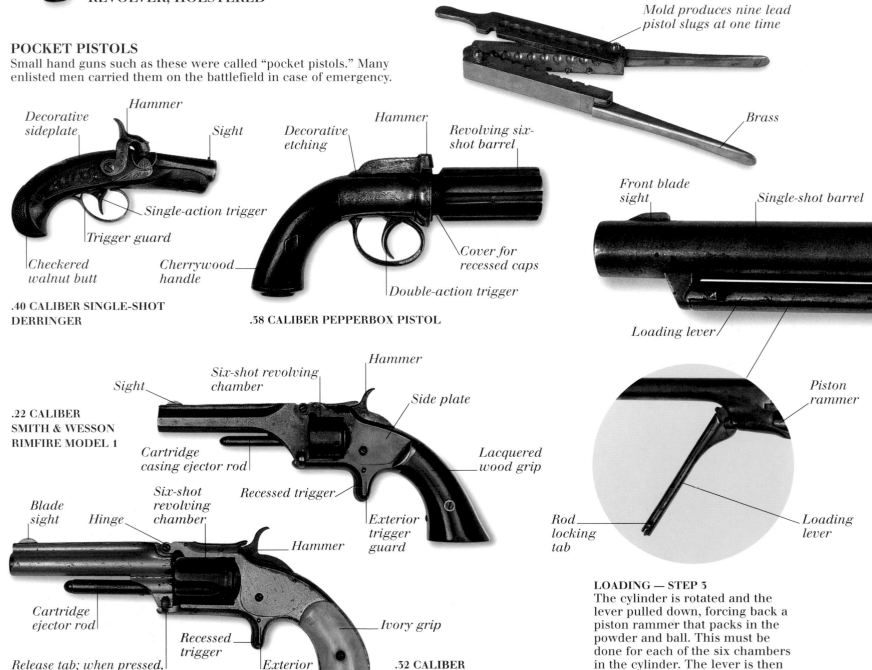

Hammer

Decorative sideplate

Sight

Single-action trigger

Trigger guard

Checkered walnut butt

Cherrywood handle

.40 CALIBER SINGLE-SHOT DERRINGER

Hammer

Decorative etching

Revolving six-shot barrel

Brass

Cover for recessed caps

Double-action trigger

.38 CALIBER PEPPERBOX PISTOL

Front blade sight

Single-shot barrel

Loading lever

.22 CALIBER SMITH & WESSON RIMFIRE MODEL 1

Sight

Six-shot revolving chamber

Hammer

Side plate

Cartridge casing ejector rod

Recessed trigger

Lacquered wood grip

Exterior trigger guard

Blade sight

Hinge

Six-shot revolving chamber

Hammer

Cartridge ejector rod

Recessed trigger

Ivory grip

Exterior trigger guard

Release tab; when pressed, it unlocks the barrel, which flips up on the hinge so the cylinder can be removed

.32 CALIBER SMITH & WESSON OLD ARMY MODEL 2

Piston rammer

Rod locking tab

Loading lever

LOADING — STEP 3

The cylinder is rotated and the lever pulled down, forcing back a piston rammer that packs in the powder and ball. This must be done for each of the six chambers in the cylinder. The lever is then returned to the locked position.

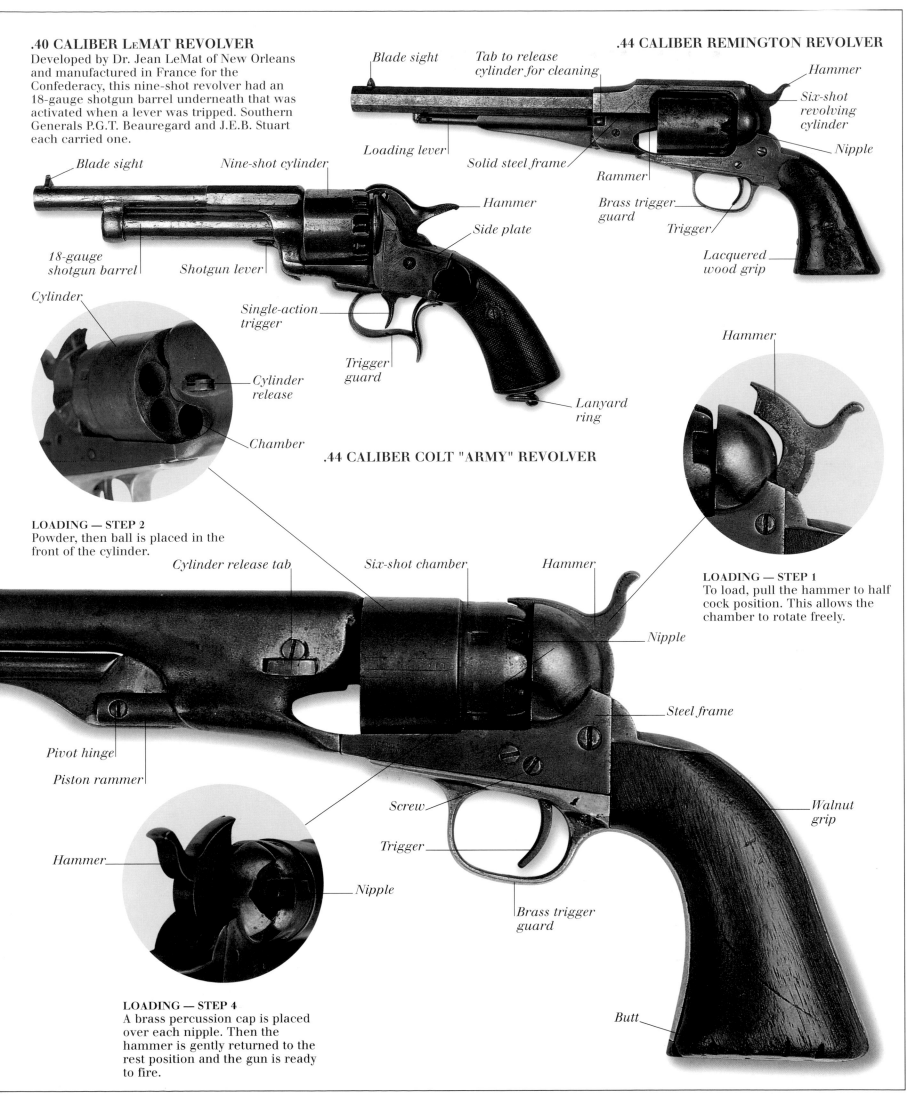

.40 CALIBER LeMAT REVOLVER

Developed by Dr. Jean LeMat of New Orleans and manufactured in France for the Confederacy, this nine-shot revolver had an 18-gauge shotgun barrel underneath that was activated when a lever was tripped. Southern Generals P.G.T. Beauregard and J.E.B. Stuart each carried one.

Blade sight

Nine-shot cylinder

Hammer

Side plate

18-gauge shotgun barrel

Shotgun lever

Single-action trigger

Trigger guard

Lanyard ring

.44 CALIBER REMINGTON REVOLVER

Blade sight

Tab to release cylinder for cleaning

Hammer

Six-shot revolving cylinder

Loading lever

Solid steel frame

Nipple

Rammer

Brass trigger guard

Trigger

Lacquered wood grip

Cylinder

Cylinder release

Chamber

LOADING — STEP 2
Powder, then ball is placed in the front of the cylinder.

Hammer

LOADING — STEP 1
To load, pull the hammer to half cock position. This allows the chamber to rotate freely.

.44 CALIBER COLT "ARMY" REVOLVER

Cylinder release tab

Six-shot chamber

Hammer

Nipple

Steel frame

Pivot hinge

Piston rammer

Screw

Trigger

Walnut grip

Hammer

Nipple

Brass trigger guard

Butt

LOADING — STEP 4
A brass percussion cap is placed over each nipple. Then the hammer is gently returned to the rest position and the gun is ready to fire.

Blades

THE AMERICAN CIVIL WAR MAY HAVE BEEN THE LAST large conflict in world history where soldiers seriously used edged weapons for attack and defense. Bowie knives, bayonets, and swords all saw some service. The bayonet was the most common military blade, and generally came in two types: the steel sword bayonet and the iron angular "tent peg" bayonet. For personal defense, no blade was more popular than the Bowie knife. Because of the reach and accuracy of their rifles, however, infantrymen rarely got close enough to an enemy to take him out with a blade. Cavalrymen, on the other hand, were expected to do this. It was their mission to pursue enemy units fleeing the battlefield and cut individual soldiers down with their sabers. A cavalry saber was a hefty weapon, and the weight enabled a mounted soldier to bring his saber down like an axe on the head and shoulders of retreating foot soldiers. Many Union blades came from the Ames Manufacturing Co. of Massachusetts. Confederates imported swords and bayonets, and also looked to local manufacturers such as the firm Leech & Rigdon of Memphis, Tennessee, to produce some.

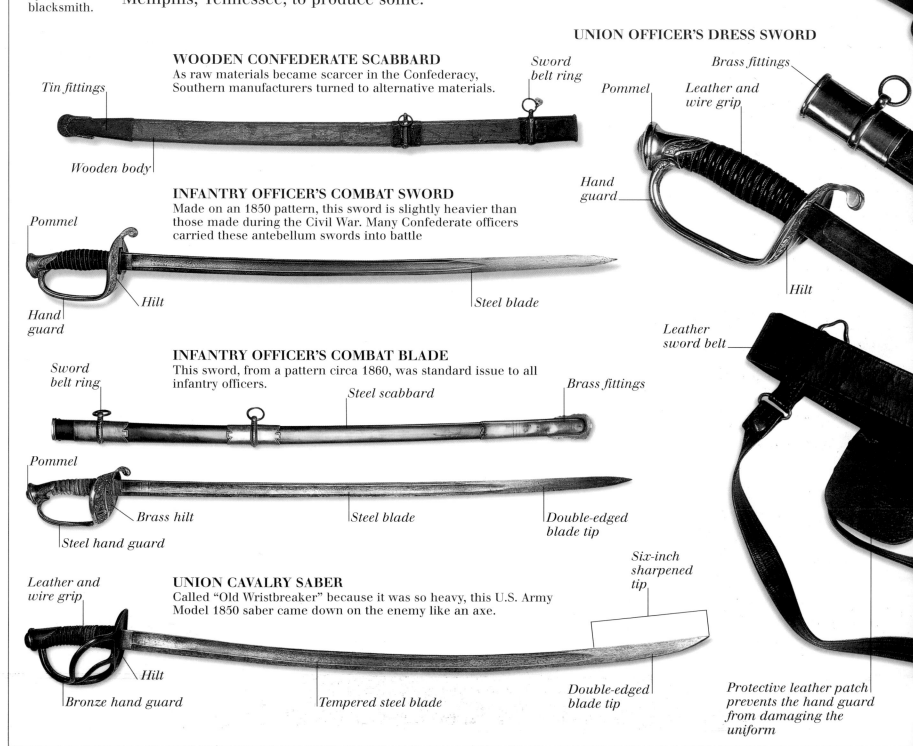

UNION OFFICER'S DRESS SWORD

Brass fittings

Pommel

Leather and wire grip

Hand guard

Hilt

Leather sword belt

WOODEN CONFEDERATE SCABBARD
As raw materials became scarcer in the Confederacy, Southern manufacturers turned to alternative materials.

Sword belt ring

Tin fittings

Wooden body

INFANTRY OFFICER'S COMBAT SWORD
Made on an 1850 pattern, this sword is slightly heavier than those made during the Civil War. Many Confederate officers carried these antebellum swords into battle

Pommel

Hilt

Hand guard

Steel blade

INFANTRY OFFICER'S COMBAT BLADE
This sword, from a pattern circa 1860, was standard issue to all infantry officers.

Sword belt ring

Steel scabbard

Brass fittings

Pommel

Brass hilt

Steel blade

Double-edged blade tip

Steel hand guard

Six-inch sharpened tip

UNION CAVALRY SABER
Called "Old Wristbreaker" because it was so heavy, this U.S. Army Model 1850 saber came down on the enemy like an axe.

Leather and wire grip

Hilt

Bronze hand guard

Tempered steel blade

Double-edged blade tip

Protective leather patch prevents the hand guard from damaging the uniform

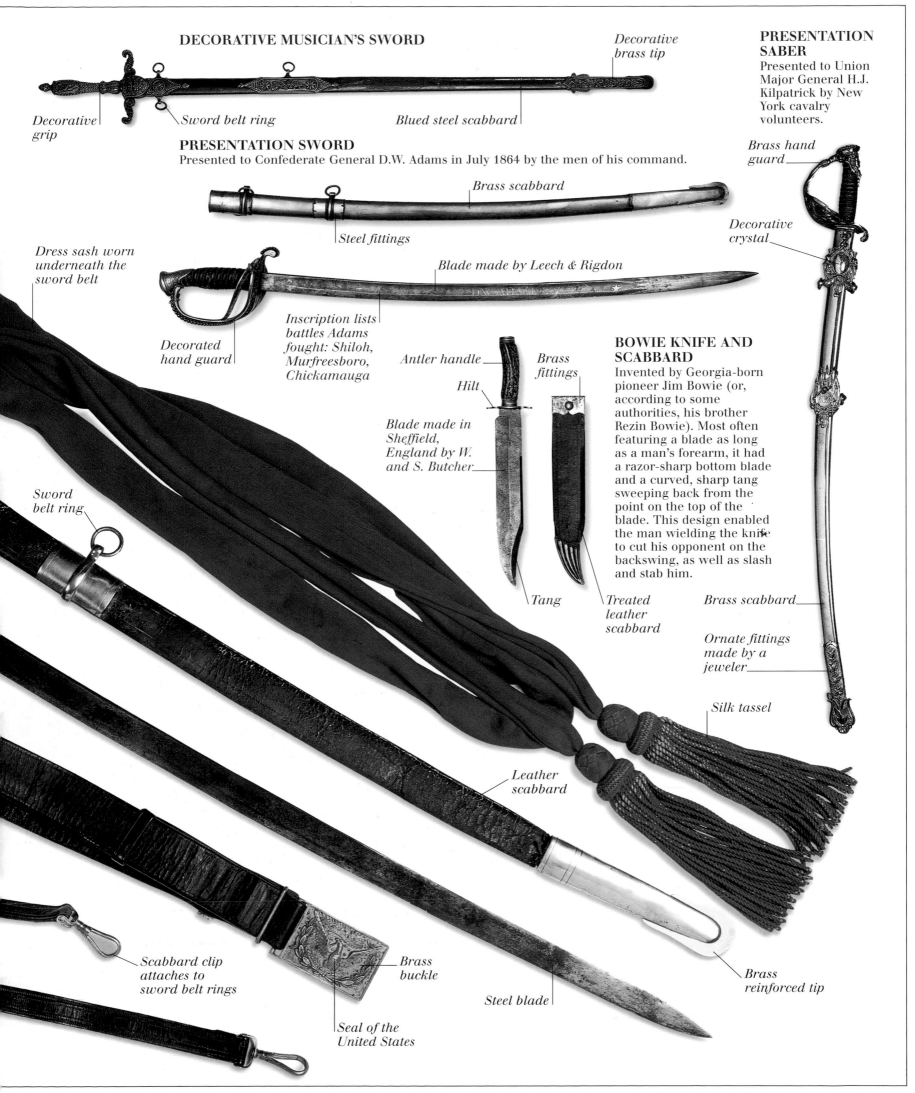

DECORATIVE MUSICIAN'S SWORD

Decorative brass tip

Decorative grip

Sword belt ring

Blued steel scabbard

PRESENTATION SWORD
Presented to Confederate General D.W. Adams in July 1864 by the men of his command.

Brass scabbard

Steel fittings

Dress sash worn underneath the sword belt

Blade made by Leech & Rigdon

Decorated hand guard

Inscription lists battles Adams fought: Shiloh, Murfreesboro, Chickamauga

PRESENTATION SABER
Presented to Union Major General H.J. Kilpatrick by New York cavalry volunteers.

Brass hand guard

Decorative crystal

BOWIE KNIFE AND SCABBARD
Invented by Georgia-born pioneer Jim Bowie (or, according to some authorities, his brother Rezin Bowie). Most often featuring a blade as long as a man's forearm, it had a razor-sharp bottom blade and a curved, sharp tang sweeping back from the point on the top of the blade. This design enabled the man wielding the knife to cut his opponent on the backswing, as well as slash and stab him.

Antler handle

Brass fittings

Hilt

Blade made in Sheffield, England by W. and S. Butcher

Tang

Treated leather scabbard

Sword belt ring

Brass scabbard

Ornate fittings made by a jeweler

Silk tassel

Leather scabbard

Scabbard clip attaches to sword belt rings

Brass buckle

Brass reinforced tip

Steel blade

Seal of the United States

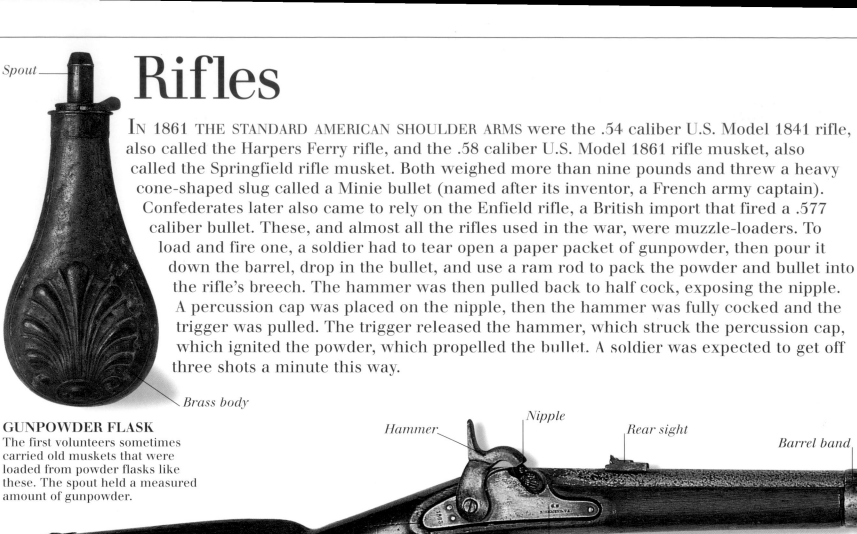

Spout

Brass body

Rifles

IN 1861 THE STANDARD AMERICAN SHOULDER ARMS were the .54 caliber U.S. Model 1841 rifle, also called the Harpers Ferry rifle, and the .58 caliber U.S. Model 1861 rifle musket, also called the Springfield rifle musket. Both weighed more than nine pounds and threw a heavy cone-shaped slug called a Minie bullet (named after its inventor, a French army captain). Confederates later also came to rely on the Enfield rifle, a British import that fired a .577 caliber bullet. These, and almost all the rifles used in the war, were muzzle-loaders. To load and fire one, a soldier had to tear open a paper packet of gunpowder, then pour it down the barrel, drop in the bullet, and use a ram rod to pack the powder and bullet into the rifle's breech. The hammer was then pulled back to half cock, exposing the nipple. A percussion cap was placed on the nipple, then the hammer was fully cocked and the trigger was pulled. The trigger released the hammer, which struck the percussion cap, which ignited the powder, which propelled the bullet. A soldier was expected to get off three shots a minute this way.

GUNPOWDER FLASK
The first volunteers sometimes carried old muskets that were loaded from powder flasks like these. The spout held a measured amount of gunpowder.

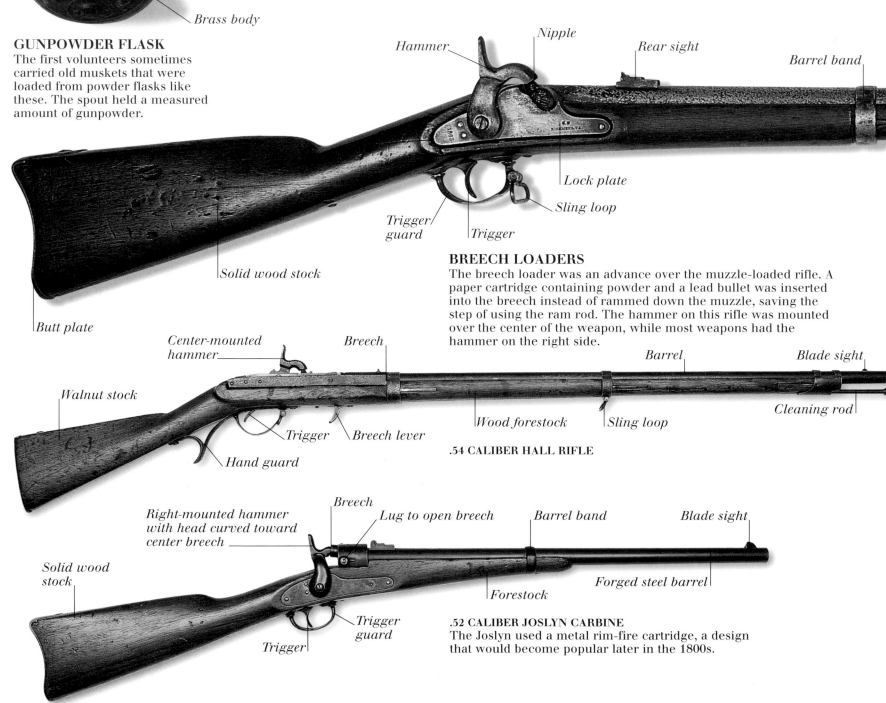

Hammer *Nipple* *Rear sight* *Barrel band*

Lock plate *Sling loop* *Trigger guard* *Trigger*

Solid wood stock

Butt plate

BREECH LOADERS
The breech loader was an advance over the muzzle-loaded rifle. A paper cartridge containing powder and a lead bullet was inserted into the breech instead of rammed down the muzzle, saving the step of using the ram rod. The hammer on this rifle was mounted over the center of the weapon, while most weapons had the hammer on the right side.

Center-mounted hammer *Breech* *Barrel* *Blade sight*

Walnut stock

Trigger *Breech lever* *Wood forestock* *Sling loop* *Cleaning rod*

Hand guard

.54 CALIBER HALL RIFLE

Right-mounted hammer with head curved toward center breech *Breech* *Lug to open breech* *Barrel band* *Blade sight*

Solid wood stock *Forestock* *Forged steel barrel*

Trigger guard *Trigger*

.52 CALIBER JOSLYN CARBINE
The Joslyn used a metal rim-fire cartridge, a design that would become popular later in the 1800s.

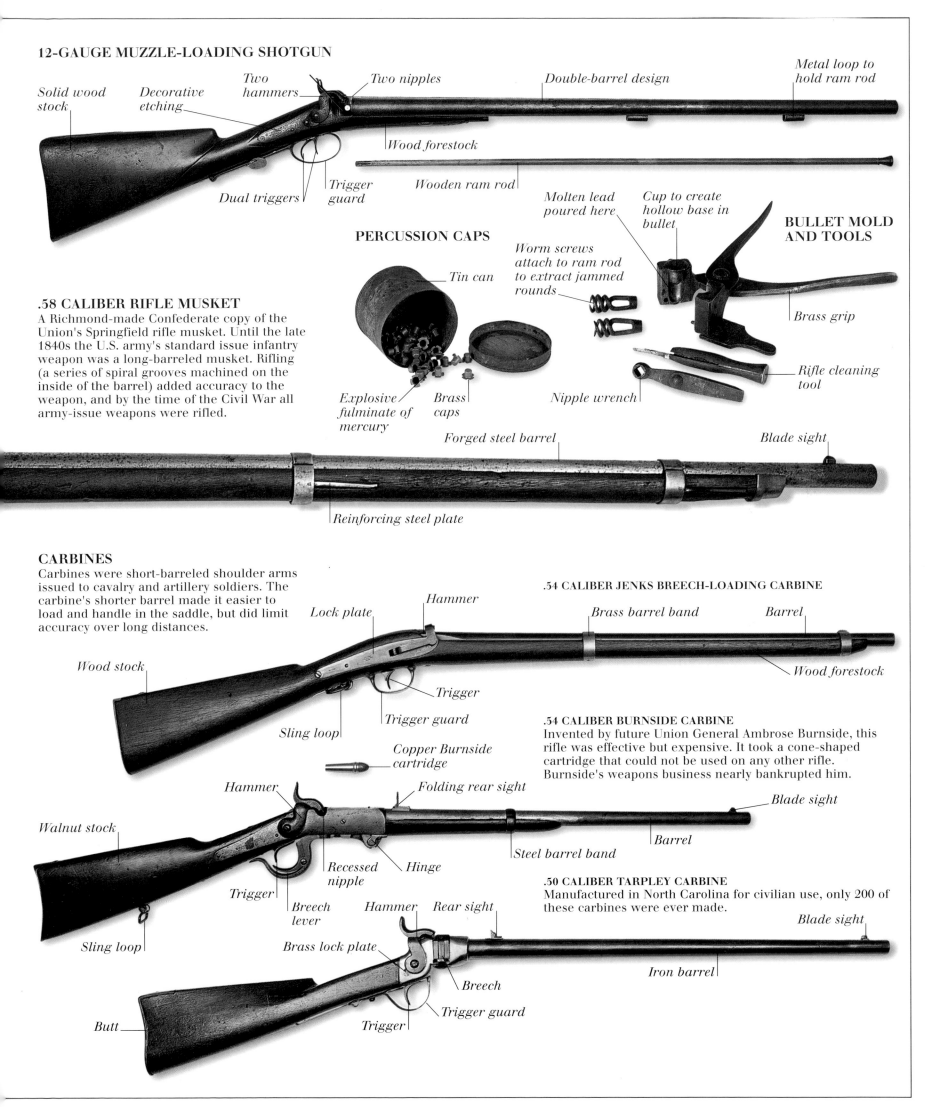

12-GAUGE MUZZLE-LOADING SHOTGUN

Solid wood stock

Decorative etching

Two hammers

Two nipples

Double-barrel design

Metal loop to hold ram rod

Wood forestock

Dual triggers

Trigger guard

Wooden ram rod

PERCUSSION CAPS

Tin can

Explosive fulminate of mercury

Brass caps

Molten lead poured here

Cup to create hollow base in bullet

Worm screws attach to ram rod to extract jammed rounds

BULLET MOLD AND TOOLS

Brass grip

Rifle cleaning tool

Nipple wrench

.58 CALIBER RIFLE MUSKET

A Richmond-made Confederate copy of the Union's Springfield rifle musket. Until the late 1840s the U.S. army's standard issue infantry weapon was a long-barreled musket. Rifling (a series of spiral grooves machined on the inside of the barrel) added accuracy to the weapon, and by the time of the Civil War all army-issue weapons were rifled.

Forged steel barrel

Blade sight

Reinforcing steel plate

CARBINES

Carbines were short-barreled shoulder arms issued to cavalry and artillery soldiers. The carbine's shorter barrel made it easier to load and handle in the saddle, but did limit accuracy over long distances.

.54 CALIBER JENKS BREECH-LOADING CARBINE

Hammer

Lock plate

Brass barrel band

Barrel

Wood stock

Trigger

Trigger guard

Sling loop

Wood forestock

.54 CALIBER BURNSIDE CARBINE

Invented by future Union General Ambrose Burnside, this rifle was effective but expensive. It took a cone-shaped cartridge that could not be used on any other rifle. Burnside's weapons business nearly bankrupted him.

Copper Burnside cartridge

Hammer

Folding rear sight

Blade sight

Walnut stock

Trigger

Recessed nipple

Hinge

Breech lever

Sling loop

Steel barrel band

Barrel

.50 CALIBER TARPLEY CARBINE

Manufactured in North Carolina for civilian use, only 200 of these carbines were ever made.

Hammer

Rear sight

Blade sight

Brass lock plate

Breech

Iron barrel

Butt

Trigger

Trigger guard

The big guns

Two-inch bore · Steel barrel · Barrel mount · Revolving cam · Loading and firing crank

CIVIL WAR CANNON WERE DIVIDED into three general classifications. First there was field artillery, the guns strapped to wheeled carriages and hauled into battle by draft horses. Next came heavy artillery, the large-bore guns found in forts defending inland cities such as Washington, D.C., and Richmond, Virginia. Then there was the seacoast artillery, the very big guns that heaved shells as heavy as loaded wagons. The most common field piece was the "Napoleon" or Model 1857 gun-howitzer. Almost as popular was the three-inch ordinance rifle (the inches referred to the gun's bore diameter), an iron gun with a rifled tube that sent shells flying on a straight, accurate trajectory. Also popular were Parrott rifles, rifled iron guns named for West Point, New York, foundry technologist Robert Parker Parrott, and – in the Confederate army – Blakely guns, imported from Britain. There was scant design difference between heavy artillery and seacoast artillery, guns called Dahlgrens (after inventor and U.S. admiral John A. Dahlgren), Rodman smoothbores (after General Thomas Jackson Rodman), Columbiads (large, smoothbore antebellum-era guns), and Armstrong guns (English imports used by Confederates).

WILLIAMS RAPID-FIRE GUN
Experiments at the Tredegar Iron Works in Richmond, Virginia, produced innovative Confederate weapons such as this light, steel, two-inch bore, breech-loading gun able to fire up to 20 one-pound shots per minute with a hand crank. Limited manufacturing capacity and demand kept Southerners from producing more than a few.

1857 GUN-HOWITZER, "NAPOLEON"
A smoothbore cannon made of brass, the Napoleon was named for French Emperor Louis Napoleon, a patron of military science.

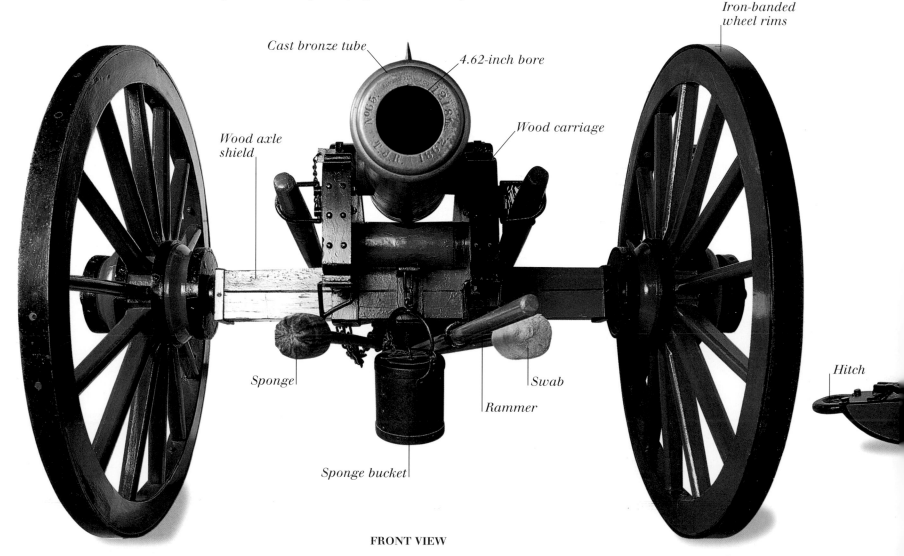

Iron-banded wheel rims

Cast bronze tube · 4.62-inch bore

Wood axle shield

Wood carriage

Sponge

Swab

Rammer

Sponge bucket

Hitch

FRONT VIEW

RODMAN GUNS

Union General Thomas Rodman developed a method of casting cannon around a hollow core, kept cool by a stream of water, that made the metal very strong. The largest had a 20-inch bore, and many 15- and 13-inch Rodman guns saw action.

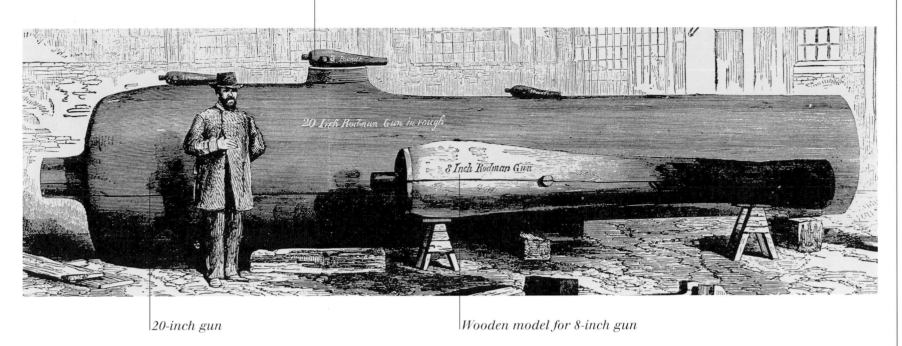

Model Rodman

20-inch gun

Wooden model for 8-inch gun

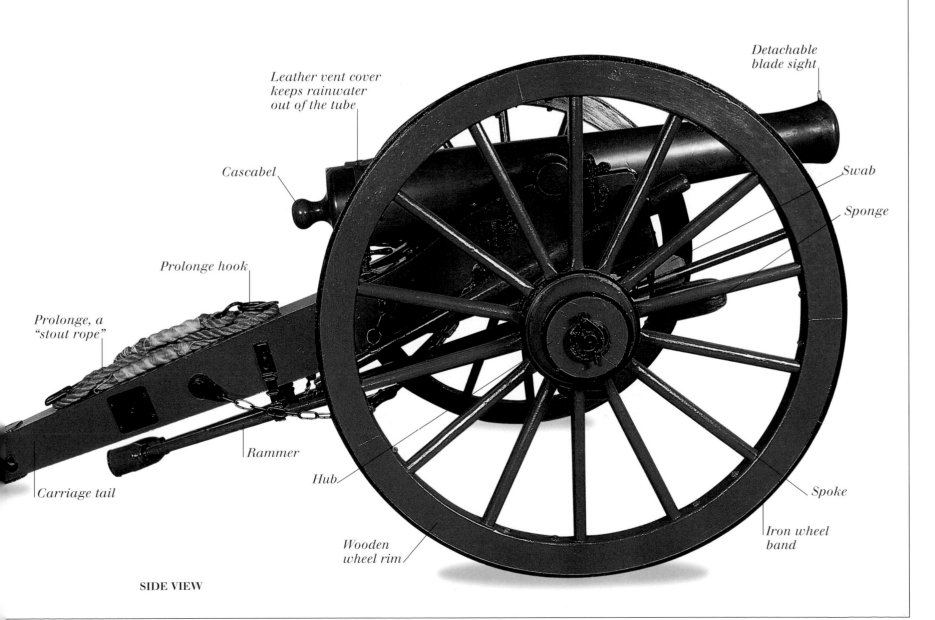

Detachable blade sight

Leather vent cover keeps rainwater out of the tube

Cascabel

Swab

Sponge

Prolonge hook

Prolonge, a "stout rope"

Rammer

Carriage tail

Hub

Spoke

Wooden wheel rim

Iron wheel band

SIDE VIEW

Firing the cannons

AMERICA'S CLASH BETWEEN NORTH AND SOUTH was the last large conflict in the world fought with muzzle-loading artillery. Not long after the Civil War ended, the great guns that once pulverized Charleston and Vicksburg, that turned bastions like Fort Sumter into rubble, started showing up in city parks as memorials – items as obsolete and harmless as windmills. The armies of Europe and the Americas dropped them in favor of breech-loading artillery. In the 1860s, however, at the peak of their development, muzzle-loading cannon were powerful enough to send an 1,080-pound shell flying 3.5 miles and versatile enough to be used as enormous shotguns against charging troops. To fire a cannon, a bag of powder was inserted into the muzzle, then the shot was loaded. Both were rammed down. Then a metal needle was thrust into a vent on the top of the barrel to make a hole in the powder bag, and a fuse was inserted into the vent. The fuse was lit, and ignited the powder. The explosion of the powder bag inside the cannon propelled the shot.

SHELL WRENCH
This wrench was used to screw in metal fuse plugs on shells for very large navy guns.

SPONGING OUT THE CANNON

Sponge | Barbette platform | Using the thumbstall

Tanned leather

ARTILLERYMAN'S THUMBSTALL
The thumbstall is a cover the gunner wore to protect his thumb from burns. He pressed his covered thumb over the sizzling hot vent hole at the breech of a cannon that had just been fired. This cut off air to the breech while it was being swabbed with a wet sponge, killing any sparks that could set off the next powder charge.

Hole for a leather thong to bind the thumbstall to the wrist

TAKE AIM
The sight and level were delicate instruments, and were removed from the gun when it wasn't in use.

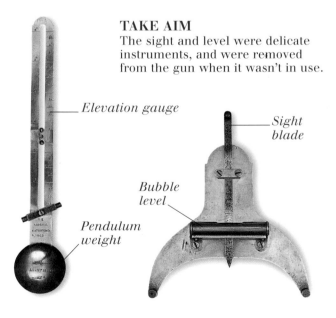

Elevation gauge

Pendulum weight

Sight blade

Bubble level

Adjusting screw

Eyepiece

Leather carrying case

PENDULUM HAUSSE TO LEVEL THE GUN

BRASS SIGHT

BINOCULARS OF CONFEDERATE GENERAL ALFRED MOUTON

SHELLS AND SHOT

A cannon like the Napoleon could fire solid iron shot, hollow case shot with a time fuse, or canister — literally a can filled with lead slugs and sawdust that acted like a large shotgun load.

Flat, armor-punching head

Hollow was filled with gunpowder and iron balls

Band that expanded to fit the gun's rifling

Iron balls

Cast iron

Flanges to fit rifling

CASE SHOT WITH IRON BALLS

SHELLS FOR RIFLED GUNS

Bolt round, used against ironclads

Solid iron ball

The sabot bands blow off when the shot is fired

Iron sabot band

Wood sabot

Thin tin cover

Tin canister

CANISTER WITH LEAD SLUGS

Lead canister rounds

12-POUND SOLID SHOT

FUSES

Timed fuses were set into fuse plugs that were inserted into hollow shells and shot. Field commanders discovered it was most useful to detonate hollow shells and shot over the heads of approaching troops, raining jagged fragments on the soldiers, so the fuses were timed to set off a charge inside the shell just as it was descending.

Time delay of fuse

Paper fuses could be cut to the desired time

Quarter-second marks

Pewter threads

BORMANN ARTILLERY FUSE
Made of pewter, this fuse screwed into the nose of a shell. The fuse had a powder charge that was ignited when the cannon was fired. Marks on the face indicate quarter seconds, up to five seconds total. A gunner would puncture the face on the quarter second he wanted the shell to detonate.

Fuse package

Soft metal exterior

PAPER TIME FUSES
When a gun was fired, sparks from the powder charge lit the fuse in the flying shell.

FUSE PLUGS

Timed fuses were set into fuse plugs that were inserted into hollow shells and shot.

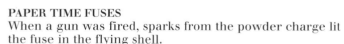

Paper fuse was inserted into the hollow

Threads screwed into shell nose

Rammed into shell nose

METAL FUSE PLUGS

WOODEN FUSE PLUG

Camp life

AFTER FOUR YEARS OF FIGHTING, SOME SOLDIERS could count on their fingers the number of times they had slept in a bed or eaten at a table. Others, mostly officers, followed the Victorian impulse to cart various home furnishings around the country with them, eating and sleeping in relative comfort. In all cases, troops showed ingenuity in adapting to a way of life that resembled an endless camping trip. Soldiers on campaign bivouacked (slept on the ground) or slept in two-man shelter tents or larger squad tents that held four to eight men. They cooked their own food over open fires. Their staple food on campaign was hardtack. This was frequently supplemented with fatty pork or bacon. Fruit and vegetables were a treat. Armies did little campaigning in the winter months. In the mountains of the South there was snow and bitter cold, and elsewhere the weather was raw and rainy, so the Union and Confederate armies would go into winter quarters. The men built log huts or lean-to's furnished with crude bunks. They huddled around fires when they were off duty, and ate meals prepared by army cooks and bakers working out of large, portable field kitchens.

STANDARD LEATHER KNAPSACK

Cap cover

Linen neck cloth

Stopper and chain

UNION SOLDIER'S METAL CANTEEN

Stenciled unit identification

Cork stopper

HAVELOCK
A cloth cover for an infantry cap, the havelock was supposed to protect the neck from the sun. Instead, soldiers used them as coffee filters or rags.

Arm strap

Coffee

Canvas cover soaked in water kept the canteen cool

Stamped tin plate

Bone handle

Fork and knife are printed with the slogan "For a good boy"

Hardtack, a thick, hard cracker

SOLDIER'S TIN CAMP WARE

Old military cap

Six-man squad tent

Cravat

Civilian

British deign fatigue cap

Wine bottle

Fatigue jacket

Folding chair

Colander

Blurred image; cameras required long exposure times, so these scenes were staged and often someone moved

Hand-carved pipe

Playing cards

Book of military tactics

High-topped boots favored by cavalry and artillery

Kitchen chair

Kitchen table

UNION OFFICERS IN CAMP

CONFEDERATE MONEY
$11, a Confederate Private's monthly pay

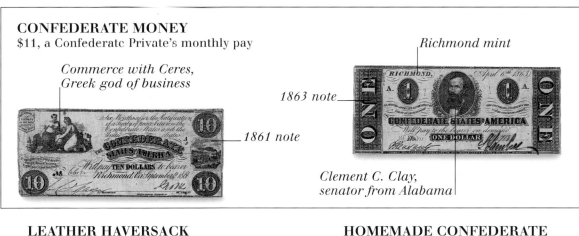

Commerce with Ceres, Greek god of business

1861 note

Richmond mint

1863 note

Clement C. Clay, senator from Alabama

CANVAS HAVERSACK
A haversack was a catch-all bag carried by infantrymen and artillerymen. The owner's unit was usually stenciled onto the bag. This haversack was carried by Confederate Captain C.L.C. DuPuy.

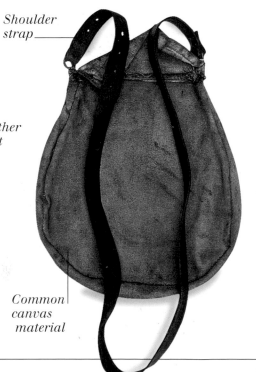

Shoulder strap

Common canvas material

LEATHER HAVERSACK

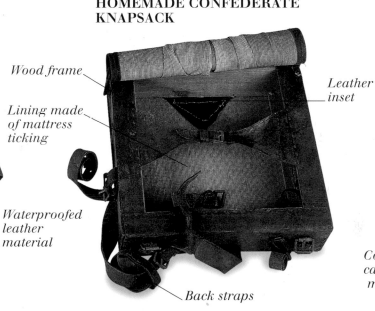

Waterproof lining

HOMEMADE CONFEDERATE KNAPSACK

Wood frame

Lining made of mattress ticking

Leather inset

Waterproofed leather material

Back straps

Personal articles

IN BOTH ARMIES THE BIG CAMP PASTIMES were letter writing, reading, gambling, wood carving (there was a fad for hand carving pipes and simple pieces of jewelry), and sometimes, drinking. Licensed vendors called "sutlers" followed the armies, selling soldiers everything from writing paper and Bibles to candy, tobacco, and whiskey. Photographers tagged along, supporting themselves by taking formal portraits of soldiers that could be sent home to their families. Chaplains also traveled with the troops to provide religious services, and late in the war in the Confederate army fundamentalist revivals became very popular. Almost all this activity took place under the open sky. The business of army life also required clerks and secretaries, men who hand wrote and filed officer's orders and filled out forms. Working from lap desks or larger tables or desks transported on army wagons, they and their officers saw to it that camp life ran on schedule and by the rules.

Union field army clerks favored this type of desk

Well cap

Ink well

Pen with metal nib

Paper lining

CONFEDERATE SOLDIERS

ITEMS ENJOYED IN CAMP

Playing cards

Twist of chewing tobacco

Confederate sheet music

Hand-carved pipe bowl

Sulfur matches

Metal waterproof match case

Case cap

I WISH I WAS IN
DIXIE'S LAND
Written and Composed expressly for
Bryant's Minstrels
by
DAN. D. EMMETT.
Arranged for the Pianoforte by
W. L. HOBBS.

NEW-YORK:
Published by FIRTH, POND & CO., No. 547 Broadway.

ANNOTATED COPY OF *HARDEE'S TACTICS*

In both the Union and Confederate armies one of the most popular books was *Hardee's Tactics*, a training manual written before the war by U.S. officer William J. Hardee, who later became a Confederate general. It and other manuals dictated drills, maneuvers, how and where tents were to be pitched, horses picketed, latrines dug, hay stored, and so on. Copies of these books were found in all camps.

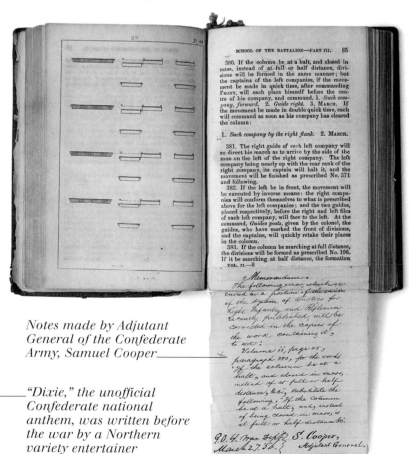

Notes made by Adjutant General of the Confederate Army, Samuel Cooper

"Dixie," the unofficial Confederate national anthem, was written before the war by a Northern variety entertainer

FAMILY PHOTO

Carried by a soldier, this photo was found on the Port Hudson, Louisiana, battlefield.

Daguerrotype image

Cardboard matte

Broken hinge; this case came with a leather cover

SOLDIER'S "HOUSEWIFE"

Soldiers were responsible for maintaining their own uniforms, and carried these sewing kits in their bags.

Thread spool

Extra button

Patching cloth

Thimble

WHISKEY FLASK

This flask was carried by Confederate Colonel J.B. Richardson of New Orleans' Washington Artillery.

Screw-on cap

Cup doubles as a cover

Finished steel

GOLD POCKET WATCH

This is Confederate Brigadier General Harry Hay's English-made watch. Watches were not common during the Civil War. It would be years before standard times zones were established and military men synchronized their attacks by the clock.

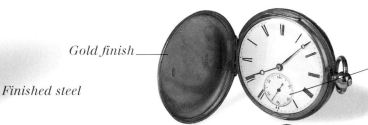

Gold finish

Second hand

Winding lever

A UNION SOLDIER'S LAP DESK

Finger cover

Fabric-covered wooden slats; this construction gave soldiers a surface to write on that could later be rolled up and stashed in a knapsack

Soldier's letter home, dated September 29, 1862

Postmark

Storage space for writing materials

Pencil

Pocket-size photograph of a loved one

Nib cover

Pen nibs

Patriotic stationary

Medicine

IF A SOLDIER WAS WOUNDED, INJURED, or seriously ill, the outlook was grim. Antibiotics such as penicillin were unknown, surgeon's tools were not sterilized, and simple sanitation and antiseptic measures were rare. Anesthetics were limited to chloroform, ether, whiskey, and sometimes the relatively new drug morphine. Common diseases such as mumps and measles decimated army camps, killing large numbers of soldiers each year. Early in the war dysentery, cholera, and malaria took entire regiments off the field. Both the Union and Confederate armies had organized Medical Departments that assigned surgeons to regiments and supplied them with surgical instruments, medicines, and chemicals. Most nurses were soldiers or male civilian volunteers. In battle, musicians and cooks were routinely detailed to serve as stretcher-bearers. Ambulances were simple wagons with poor suspension – vehicles that jostled the badly injured as they moved over farm fields and rutted roads. During battles or campaigns they delivered the wounded to private homes and farm buildings that were seized for use as hospitals and surgeries. Dining room and kitchen tables ended up serving as operating tables.

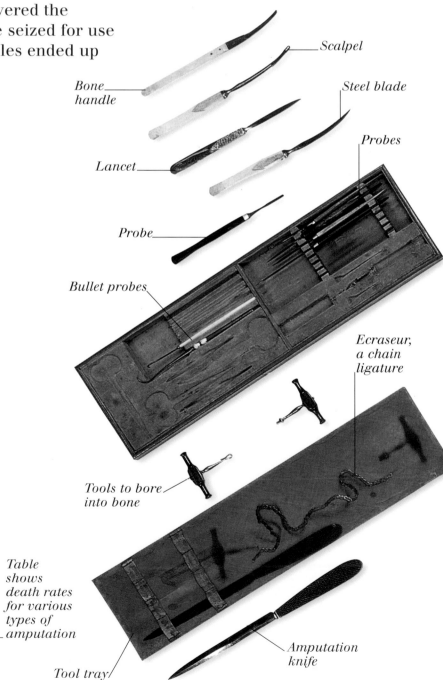

CONFEDERATE ARMY MEDICAL DISABILITY CERTIFICATE
Surgical patients who survived their procedures and a few days in a field hospital were eventually shipped to permanent hospitals in cities far behind the front lines.

Original enlistment information

Doctor's certification of disability

Scalpel

Bone handle

Steel blade

Lancet

Probes

Probe

Bullet probes

Ecraseur, a chain ligature

Tools to bore into bone

Table shows death rates for various types of amputation

Amputation knife

Tool tray

UNION SURGEONS AT WORK IN A TENT HOSPITAL

Wooden operating table

GRUESOME STATISTICS FROM A CONFEDERATE ARMY MEDICAL MANUAL
Amputation was the most common form of surgery, and many patients did not survive the procedure.

B. CONSOLIDATED TABLE

Of Capital Operations performed in and around Richmond, Va., from June 1st to August 1st, 1862, in C. S. Hosp'l.

AMPUTATION OF LEG.

PERIOD IN WHICH OPERATED UPON.	Upper third.		Middle third.		Lower third.		Not stated.		Total No. of operations.	Grand total of operations.	Died.		Total of deaths.	Recovered or Convalescent.		Total recovered or convalescent.	Per centage of Deaths.		Total per centage of Deaths.
	Circular.	Flap. Not stated.	Circular.	Flap. Not stated.	Circular.	Flap. Not stated.	Circular.	Flap. Not stated.	Circular. Flap. Not stated.		Circular.	Flap. Not stated.		Circular.	Flap. Not stated.	Circular.	Flap. Not stated.	
Primary,	9 2 30	3 3 2 3	2	18 16 9	47	72	8 2 19 29	12 3 28 43	50	22 40⁴	41
No. of deaths.	5 12	2 2 1	1	8 8 2	19	29					
Intermediary,	5 3 12	1 1	4	4 6 4	20	30	2 2 8 12	4 2 12 18	33	50 40	40
No. of deaths.	1 1 7	2		1 3 1	8	12					
Secondary,	2 4 7	2		14 4 4	22	30	3 4 17	1 12 13	75	100 45⁴	56⁵
No. of deaths.	2 4 3	1		7 3 4	10	17					
Aggregate,	16 9 49	6 5 4 2	4 7	36 26 17	89	132	13 8 37 58	17 5 52 74	50	47 44	43⁹
Ratio of deaths.	58 56 42⁶	60 75 50 25	16	41 50 47 41⁴	41⁴	43⁹					

APPENDIX.

394

ARMY SURGICAL TOOLS

Aside from herbal medicines, bandages and splints, some narcotics, and dietary supplements, Confederate and Union doctors found their most reliable tools were ghastly looking surgical instruments such as bone saws, amputation knives, scalpels, clamps, tourniquets, and a variety of sewing needles, sutures, bullet probes, and extractors.

Page from a Union army surgeon's manual

Forward hand grip

Bone saw

Bullet extractor

Bone crimper

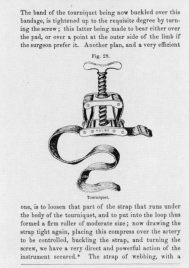

APPLICATION OF DRESSINGS. 41

A SURGEON'S GUIDE TO REMOVING BULLETS

TOURNIQUET
This instrument was used to staunch blood flow during amputations.

Wooden case

Rachitome

Probe

Hatchet edge for cutting away bone

Surgeon's "mallet"

Gutta percha wrapped grip

Bone grip

Tourniquet

Bone tool

Set of amputation knives

Surgical saw

Bone cutter

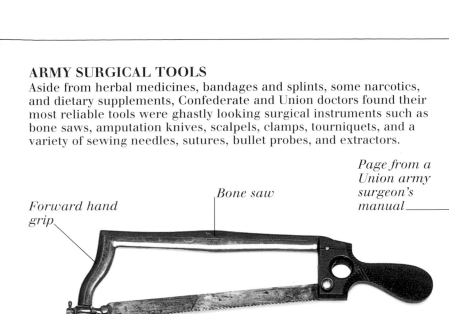

Slavery

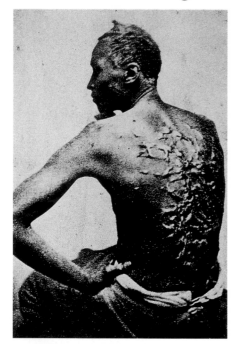

ESCAPED SLAVE
Gordon was photographed by a Union army surgeon in Baton Rouge, Louisiana, in 1863. He later served as a corporal in the Union army.

SLAVERY IN THE UNITED STATES WAS NOT THE cause of the Civil War. The main issues were states' rights, the question of whether or not a state could nullify its compact with the Federal government, and the legality of seizing U.S. property inside state lines. But slavery brought those issues to a head. Lawmakers in slave states created Black Codes - rules that defined the slave's place in Southern society and pressed all whites to look to their enforcement. Slaves, for instance, could not travel after dark in most places, and were prohibited from learning to read and write. Except during religious services, slaves could not assemble without white supervision. These rules were upheld with force by frightened whites; the slave population in South Carolina and Mississippi, for instance, was far larger than the free white population. Calls for abolition won political support in the late 1850s and prompted national legislators to restrict the westward expansion of slavery. Angry and defiant, Southerners resisted these measures, until Abraham Lincoln's 1860 election to the Presidency goaded them into secession. They believed their economic way of life had no future in an abolitionist United States. Ironically, slavery continued to be legal throughout Lincoln's lifetime in any state that remained in the Union. The Emancipation Proclamation, which became effective January 1, 1863, freed only the slaves residing in territories that were in rebellion. Slavery was not completely outlawed until passage of the 13th Amendment to the Constitution in 1865 - on December 18, after the war was over.

SLAVE QUARTERS
These quarters were built by the slaves themselves. Their master was exceptional, giving them quality building supplies for their cabins. Most slaves' cabins were slapped together with shoddy materials, providing little shelter from the rain and cold. Unless they had duties inside the master's home, slaves were expected to stay within the confines of the slave quarters or in the master's fields.

Path to master's house

Main gate

Wash tub

Mounted overseer

Common building for storing tools

Brick chimneys

BILL OF SALE

Few slave holders could afford such a large purchase. While there were 385,000 slave holders in the South at the 1860 census, more than 50 percent owned fewer than five slaves.

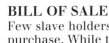

Age

Name

Price

Copper bell; slaves who grew tired of hearing the bells muffled the clappers with dirt and mud

Hand-forged iron collar

Iron hinge

SLAVE COLLAR

This and other items used to discipline or restrain black men and women were made by slave blacksmiths at their masters' direction. This collar was made to be worn by a slave who had previously run away or was considered likely to run away. The bells always alerted the master to the slave's location.

POSTER ANNOUNCING SLAVE AUCTION

The U.S. Congress' 1807 ban on the importation of slaves spawned a lucrative trade in slave smuggling, slave breeding, and interstate slave dealing. In the late 1850s, by one estimate, an average of 80,000 slaves were traded in the United States each year, at a value of $60 million.

Solid steel door

Open tops of cells enabled buyers to look down in the cell at the slave for sale without opening the door

Dead bolt

Iron barred door

Mule stable

Description implies the slaves are strong field hands

Auctioneer; auctioning slaves was a specialty for some auctioneering professionals

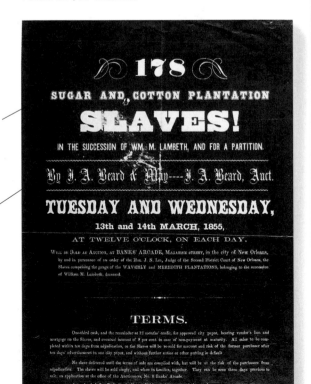

VIRGINIA DEALER'S SLAVE PEN

The American slave's miserable lot - to be denied status as a human being, to be bought and sold on an auction block like a farm animal, to be forced to breed, to be separated from a spouse and children by a sale that profited the master, to be beaten or killed at a master's direction, to be worked night and day with no more compensation than a meager meal and ragged cast-off clothes, to live and die as property - was determined by economics.

Prisoners of war

EARLY IN THE WAR, IF AN ARMY CAPTURED a large number of enemy soldiers they disarmed them and granted them battlefield parole. The prisoners were permitted to go home on the promise that they would not take up arms again until an identical number of their enemies were given battlefield parole. This almost childlike example of trust and fair play did not last long. Although the parole system remained in force through much of 1864, both the Union and Confederate armies quickly set up prisoner-of-war camps far behind their lines. While prisoners in all facilities suffered some deprivation, Andersonville Prison outside Plains, Georgia, was notorious. Prisoners lived in blanket shelters, shacks or holes in the ground with blanket canopies. The stream running through the camp – the only available water – carried typhus and cholera. Food was so severely rationed that huge numbers of men succumbed to malnutrition and scurvy. Stronger, desperate inmates preyed on weaker ones for their meager rations or belongings. At the war's end the camp commandant, a Swiss national named Major Henry Wirz, was the only Confederate officer executed for war crimes.

STARVED SURVIVOR OF ANDERSONVILLE PRISON

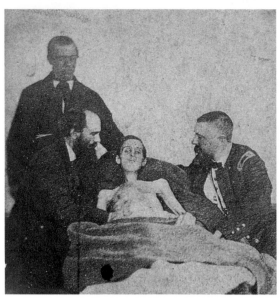

UNION SOLDIERS LIBERATED FROM CAMP FORD

Among the lock-ups for captured Union troops were Camp Ford in Tyler, Texas, Salisbury Prison in Salisbury, North Carolina, Castle Thunder and Belle Isle prisons near Richmond, Virginia, and Libby Prison on the Richmond riverfront, where Union officers were jailed.

UNION PAROLE PAPERS

Confederate gunner J.H. Forshee's parole papers, issued by his Union captors.

U.S. government processing stamp

Parole noting Forshee is part of an exchange for Union soldiers

Shade hat hand-woven by camp inmates

Transportation stamp dated April 22, 1865 – 13 days after Lee surrendered

Note written by Forshee with forget-me-not flowers

Photograph of Forshee

Provost Marshal's pass allowing Forshee to travel home

The Provost Marshal was the head of the military police

Provost Marshal's office processing stamp

Simple wooden barracks

THE ANDERSONVILLE COMPOUND

Camp guards' offices

Any inmate crossing an interior line called the "dead line," a marked line near the camp's inner fence, was liable to be shot

Polluted stream

Confederate garrison

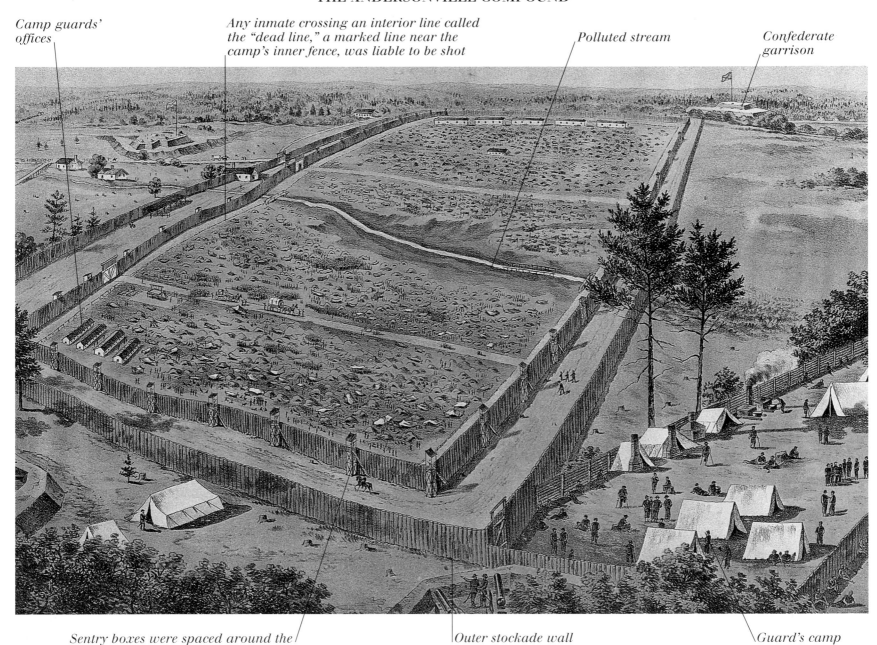

Sentry boxes were spaced around the perimeter of the interior wall

Outer stockade wall

Guard's camp

PRISONER-OF-WAR CAMP AT ELMIRA

Southerners were held in spots that included Elmira, New York, Johnson's Island on Lake Erie near Sandusky, Ohio, and Fort Warren in Boston Harbor – where high-ranking Southern officers and Confederate notables were jailed.

FORT DELAWARE PRISON

Constructed in the 1850s on swampy Pea Patch Island near the mouth of the Delaware River, Fort Delaware was built to defend Philadelphia from foreign invasion. When tides ran high, much of it was flooded by seawater. Disease in the damp surroundings killed approximately 2,700 Confederate prisoners.

Guarded catwalk

Parade ground

Sally port

Communications

THE AMERICAN CIVIL WAR WAS THE FIRST large conflict in world history in which both contending armies used instant telegraphic communication. By 1861 every state east of the Mississippi was linked by telegraphic cable. That April, when Confederates attacked Fort Sumter in South Carolina, word of the event was instantly sent to New York City, Washington, D.C., and points South: "Fort Sumter is fired upon." In both Union and Confederate armies, telegraphy and other forms of military communication were the responsibility of the Signal Corps. Members of these corps used Morse code and secret military codes to communicate via telegraph, and also sent messages across battlefields or long lines of march with signal flags or reflecting mirrors. In combat these corpsmen would climb trees or the roofs of houses to signal different army units, or would quickly erect flimsy signal towers out of stacked, notched logs, and signal from their tops.

SIGNAL DRUM
Drums and bugles were played on the field, signaling instructions for firing and troop movements. This one was found on the Gettysburg battlefield, and was one model in the famous painting, "The Battle of Gettysburg."

Animal hide drum head

Handpainted eagle and crest

Strapping to keep drum head taut

Polished wood key tip

Key arm

Electrical contact

Wire terminals

Spring rod

Key contact

Wooden base

PORTABLE TELEGRAPH KEY
Telegraphy was an American innovation, developed by New England artist-turned-inventor Samuel F.B. Morse. It was first demonstrated to the U.S. Congress in 1844.

Rolled canvas window blind

Sending and receiving telegraphic terminals

One of two telegrapher's desks

Telegrapher

Signal officer

ARMY FIELD TELEGRAPHER'S WAGON
This portable telegrapher's office had sending and receiving sets. It carried some office supplies and kerosene lights for work at night, and galvanic batteries to power the telegraph's electromagnets.

Insulated wire hook

Bamboo field poles for temporary hook-ups to existing heavy lines

HANGING MILITARY TELEGRAPH CABLE
During a campaign, cable had to be strung to encampments and other areas that might not have been previously wired. Army telegraph poles were often live trees stripped of limbs and bark.

Gutta percha insulated field telegraph wire

Wire spool

Field telegrapher's wagon

Sending and receiving key and letter indicator

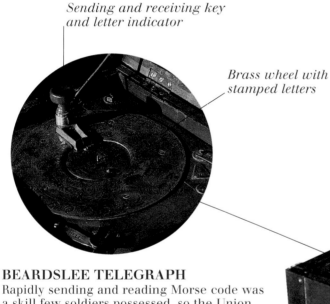

Brass wheel with stamped letters

Receiving terminals

Sending terminals

Magneto crank electrical fittings

BEARDSLEE TELEGRAPH
Rapidly sending and reading Morse code was a skill few soldiers possessed, so the Union army adopted the Beardslee telegraph. Electric impulses sent or received over the Beardslee system moved a metal arrow around a large brass wheel with the letters of the alphabet stamped on it, spelling out messages in English or secret code. The system was powered by a hand-cranked magneto, which limited the Beardslee's range to five miles.

Carrying strap

Brass fittings

Letter wheel gear mechanism

Wire wrapping

Service door

Magneto

Flags

COWAN'S MISSISSIPPI BATTERY

FLAGS WERE more than symbols of national and unit pride; they were also important elements in battlefield movement and tactics. Regimental flags marked unit positions on the field and were the targets of attacking troops. If an enemy flag was captured, the soldiers that had rallied around it fell back to the position of the nearest allied unit – a position also marked by a flag. It was expected that regiments would defend these banners to almost the last man. Several Union soldiers who seized Confederate battle flags were awarded the Medal of Honor (the only government medal awarded during the Civil War to any soldier) because they risked near-certain death to make the capture. Individual unit flags on both sides were unique and colorful, often designed and hand-sewn by the women of the community in which the company or regiment was raised, and presented to its men in a formal ceremony. The flag of the Irish Brigade in the Army of the Potomac is a famous example. Highly visible on the battlefield, it drew an enormous amount of enemy fire.

St. Andrew's Cross

Pierced by 83 bullets in a charge up Snodgrass Hill at the Battle of Chickamauga in September 1863

Cotton fabric

2ND BATTALION, HILLIARD'S ALABAMA LEGION
The blue St. Andrew's Cross on this battle flag was one of several design elements for a national flag authorized by the Confederate Congress. Two subsequent national flags featured the St. Andrew's Cross on a red canton in the upper left corner, atop a white field; a red vertical bar was added to the end of the white field in a subsequent design because several critics claimed the white flag suggested surrender.

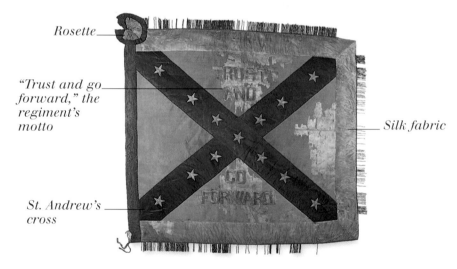

Rosette

"Trust and go forward," the regiment's motto

St. Andrew's cross

Silk fabric

25TH LOUISIANA INFANTRY

Canton

Eight stars, for the states that seceded before March 1861

Designed by Professor Nicola Marschall of Montgomery, Alabama

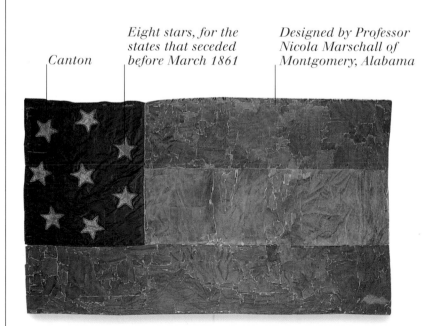

1ST LOUISIANA SPECIAL BATTALION
The first Confederate flag to be called the Stars and Bars was this design, adopted in March of 1861 at the Convention of Seceded States. This national flag was carried by Wheat's Tigers.

Canton

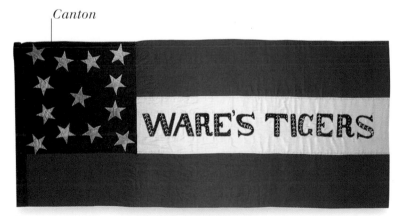

WARE'S TIGERS OF CORPUS CHRISTI, TEXAS
The stars represent states that seceded through May 1861, as well as Missouri and Kentucky – states that maintained competing Union and Confederate governments.

Indian holding bow and arrow

Star denoting Massachusetts was one of the original 13 states

Massachusetts state seal

Pennsylvania state seal

Stars represent all the states, including those that had seceded

Canton

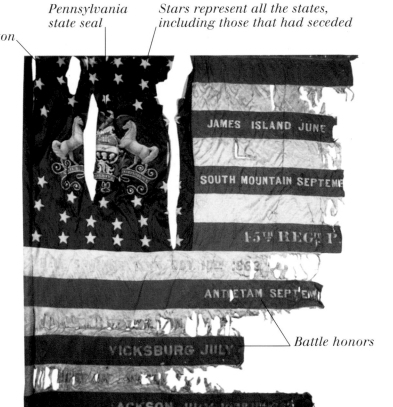

JAMES ISLAND JUNE

SOUTH MOUNTAIN SEPTEM

45ᵀᴴ REGᵗ P

ANTIETAM SEPT'EM

VICKSBURG JULY

Battle honors

JACKSON JULY 10 & 11

54TH MASSACHUSETTS VOLUNTEERS
The all-black 54th lost its officers and many of its soldiers in an assault on Fort Wagner, South Carolina.

45TH PENNSYLVANIA REGIMENT

Irish harp

Banner

Rays of light convey, "The sun always shines upon the Irish"

White horse

Bald eagle

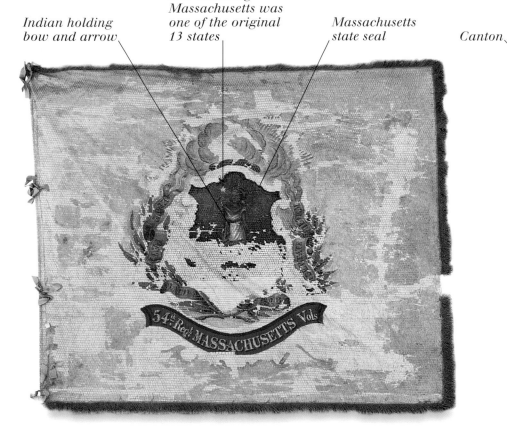

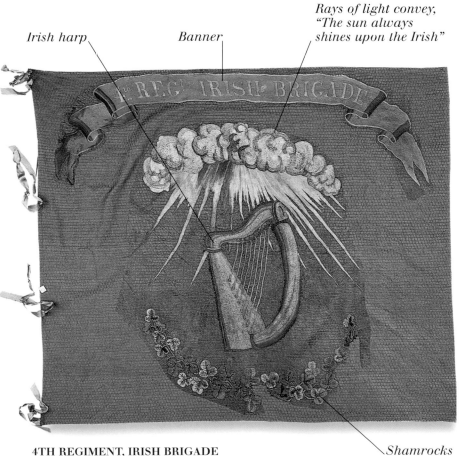

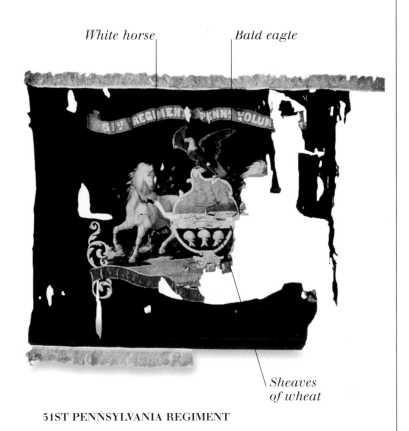

Sheaves of wheat

4TH REGIMENT, IRISH BRIGADE
This flag was carried by one of the units of the Union's Irish Brigade, which was made up of Irish immigrants and men of Irish ancestry.

Shamrocks

51ST PENNSYLVANIA REGIMENT

Railroads

CONFEDERATE RAILWAY GUN

BEFORE THE CIVIL WAR, THE U.S. government estimated that 30,000 miles of track had been laid around the nation. Most of those lines ran across the North and upper Midwest, but by 1861 every major community in the Confederacy east of the Mississippi River was linked by rail service. This would, in part, dictate military strategy and objectives: Everyone recognized that railroads were tools of war, and each army made the destruction of its enemy's railroads a high priority. Northern railroads kept the fighting fronts supplied with men, food, and equipment; Southern railroads shuffled outnumbered Confederate troops from one front to another. At the First Battle of Bull Run, Confederate forces had fought Union troops to a near standstill. At a pivotal point, the Confederates were suddenly reinforced by soldiers commanded by General Joseph E. Johnston – men who, the day before, had been in the Shenandoah Valley and had been shuttled to the battlefield by rail. Their timely arrival turned the tide in favor of the South. The obvious power of rail transport led both the Union and Confederacy to exert government control over their railroads. The U.S. army even established its own line, the U.S. Military Railroad.

"DICTATOR" MORTAR
This Union artillery piece moved around the Petersburg, Virginia, siege line perimeter on a railroad flat car, lobbing shells into the Confederates, then moving on before enemy artillery could get a fix on its position and destroy it.

200-pound shell

13-inch bore

Steps for loaders

Gun weighed 17,000 pounds

Elevating arm

RAILROAD BATTERY
This armored car was built to protect workmen on the Baltimore & Ohio Railroad. At the outbreak of the war, Southern sympathizers threatened to burn all the railroad bridges between Washington and Baltimore, to prevent Union troops from reinforcing Washington, D.C. They did not completely succeed, and after Baltimore was occupied the damage was hastily repaired.

Smokestack

Whistle

Pressure valve

Engineer's cab

Conductor's car

Tender car

Locomotive

Telegraph line

Cannon

Sheet iron casing

THE GENERAL

The most famous locomotive of the Civil War, The General, was hijacked by Union saboteur James J. Andrews and a crew of Northern volunteers. They rode this Confederate engine north from the Atlanta area, destroying the track behind them, all the while pursued by Southern railroad men and troops aboard the engine Texas. The Southerners captured Andrews and several of his men south of Ringgold, Georgia, when The General ran out of boiler water and fuel. Andrews and eight of his crew were hanged for the April 1862 hijacking.

Smokestack

Kerosene night lamp

Bell

Whistle

Pressure valve

Engineer's cab

Boiler

Right driving piston

Steam valve cover

Driving arm

Piston arm

Cow catcher

Workman's step

Left driving piston

Aerial observation

Silk balloon "Intrepid"

Lowe

Gondola

Tether line

Signal corps wagon

Tether crew

Tree stumps; trees were cleared to make way for take-offs and landings

LOWE IN HIS GONDOLA
When a mechanical winch was unavailable, it took a large crew to manage a balloon's tether. If Lowe was allowed to fly free, he was liable to be captured.

BOTH THE UNION AND the Confederacy recognized the military advantages of flight. In 1861 the U.S. War Department authorized "Professor" T.C. Lowe, a Northern balloon enthusiast, to set up a military aeronautics program and gave him a staff and a colonel's pay. Lowe came under hostile fire several times, but was able to supply the Union army with intelligence on Confederate troop movements, and could also direct artillery fire. The Confederates never organized their War Department to take up aeronautics; all Confederate balloon experiments were the responsibility of individual officers or private parties. One of the best documented examples of a Confederate military balloon ascension took place in 1862 during the Peninsula Campaign south of Richmond, Virginia. Union troops were observed by a giant silk balloon that had been built and launched by a Southern army officer, who used gas from the Richmond city gas works to get his craft aloft. During that same period another Confederate balloon was transported down Virginia's James River aboard the C.S.S. Teaser, and made several ascensions from her decks to observe Union army movements. This made the Teaser one of the first aircraft carriers.

LOWE INFLATING HIS BALLOON AT GAINES MILL, VIRGINIA
Acid dripped onto coal in the generator, creating lighter-then-air gas.

LOWE BALLOONS

Between June 1861 and May 1863, Lowe built a fleet of seven balloons, invented a portable gas generator, and had a part in more than 3,000 military balloon ascensions. This chapter in military history ended when Lowe resigned from government service following a feud with Major General Joseph Hooker. This painting by Sydney King shows Lowe at a Union camp on the Berkeley Plantation near Williamsburg, Virginia, in spring of 1862.

Berkeley Plantation house

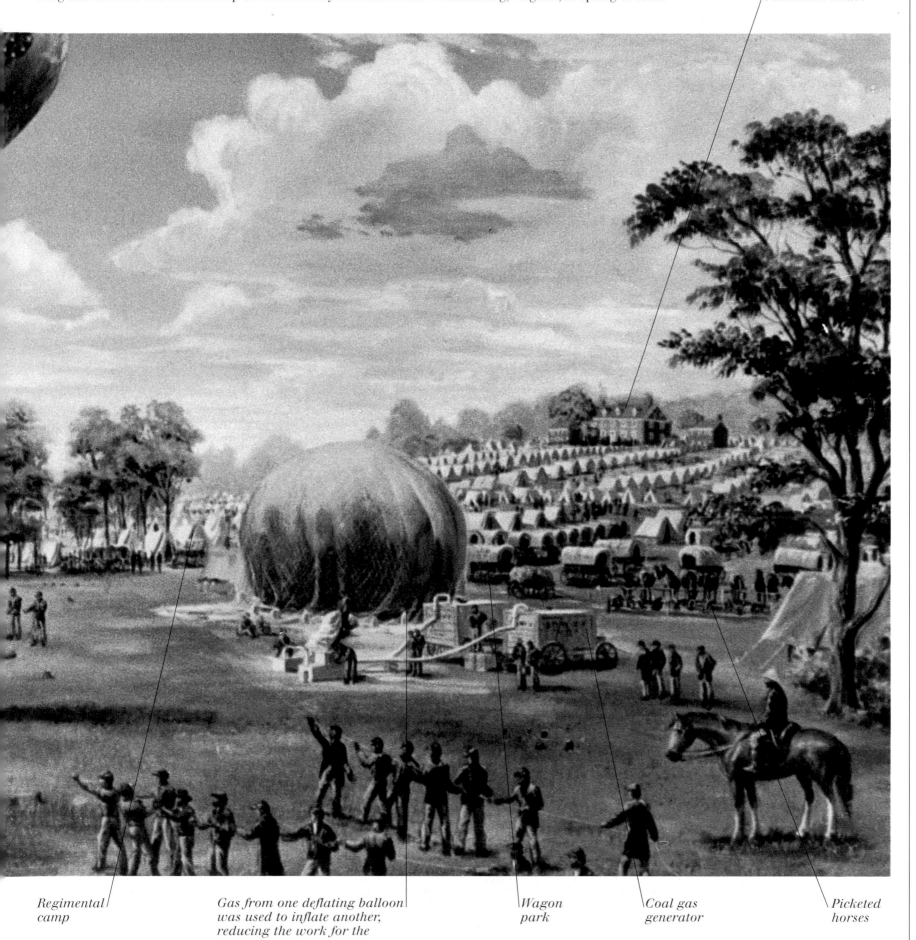

Regimental camp

Gas from one deflating balloon was used to inflate another, reducing the work for the generators

Wagon park

Coal gas generator

Picketed horses

The Monitor and the Merrimac

CANNONBALL
A souvenir of the battle between the Monitor and the Merrimac. This solid iron cannonball was flattened against the Merrimac's iron side.

IN APRIL 1861 THE COMMANDER of the U.S. navy's Gosport Navy Yard at Norfolk, Virginia, ordered the facility set on fire to keep the ships from falling into Confederate hands. One ship caught in the blaze, the U.S.S. Merrimac, burned to the water line, but its hull and engines survived. Southern naval engineers restored its steam engines, covered it with an iron casemate that reached below water level, attached an iron ram to the bow and armed it with 10 cannon. The revamped vessel was christened C.S.S. Virginia (although she was always known as the Merrimac in the North) and turned over to Confederate navy Captain Franklin Buchanan. When word of the work being done to the old Merrimac reached the North, there was great public concern. Many believed Confederates were building a super weapon that could sail up the Potomac River and shell Washington, D.C., into submission. This climate of near panic won inventor John Ericsson, a Swedish immigrant, a U.S. Government contract to build the Union an ironclad ship of its own. Christened the Monitor, Ericsson's vessel went into service February 25, 1862, and sailed out of Brooklyn, New York, for Virginia.

Full crew of 350

C.S.S. Virginia (Merrimac) armed with six Dahlgren cannons and nine rifled guns

MERRIMAC SINKING THE CUMBERLAND
On March 8, 1862, the Merrimac lead an attack on the U.S. navy blockade squadron anchored at Hampton Roads near Newport News, Virginia. She rammed and sank the U.S.S. Cumberland and shot the U.S.S. Congress to pieces. The frigate U.S.S. Minnesota was run aground, and the rest of the wooden Union fleet was helpless.

Gun port

170-foot long superstructure

Submerged four-foot cast iron ram, used to sink wooden ships

30-gun frigate U.S.S. Cumberland

Confederate
flag

Slant-sided
design with a
35-degree slope

United
States
flag

U.S.S. Monitor
armed with two 11-inch
Dahlgren cannons

Revolving
20-foot turret

Crew of 58

THE MERRIMAC AND THE MONITOR

On March 9 the Merrimac went up against the
iron-turreted Monitor, commanded by
Lieutenant John L. Worden. Lieutenant
Catesby Jones commanded the Merrimac,
after Captain Buchanan was wounded by small
arms fire the day before. Though outgunned,
the Monitor's revolving gun turret kept one of
its two Dahlgren cannons trained on the
Merrimac at all times, and the two were able
to do battle for four hours before calling off
the fight. This view of the battle was drawn by
a newspaper artist on shore.

CUTAWAY VIEW OF THE MONITOR

The Monitor became the model for a variety
of Union ironclad vessels.

CROSS-SECTION OF THE MONITOR

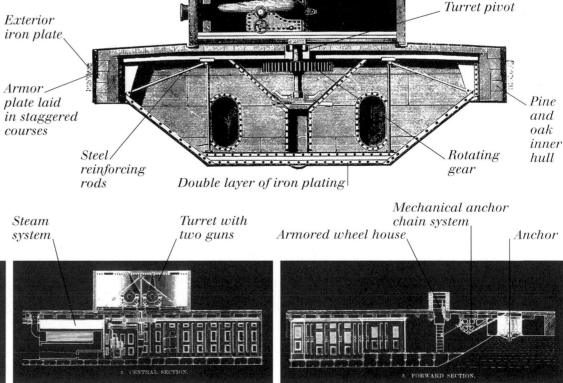

11-inch Dahlgren
cannon

Rotating iron
turret

Turret pivot

Exterior
iron plate

Armor
plate laid
in staggered
courses

Steel
reinforcing
rods

Double layer of iron plating

Rotating
gear

Pine
and
oak
inner
hull

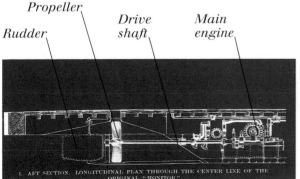

Propeller

Rudder

Drive
shaft

Main
engine

Steam
system

Turret with
two guns

Mechanical anchor
chain system

Armored wheel house

Anchor

1. AFT SECTION. LONGITUDINAL PLAN THROUGH THE CENTER LINE OF THE
ORIGINAL "MONITOR".

2. CENTRAL SECTION.

3. FORWARD SECTION.

Ironclads

C.S.S. TENNESSEE

THE CIVIL WAR promoted the transition from wooden ships to iron-clad naval vessels - the forerunners of great steel fighting ships that are part of every navy today. The stalemate between the Monitor and the Merrimac showed the Union the necessity of starting up armored ship production. A series of Monitor-model vessels were produced for combat along the coastline, and armor was added to a variety of vessels used in naval battle along the western rivers. Some of the Union's better-known ironclad riverboats were the Indianola and the Cairo. Both were sunk in action. The Confederate navy, which was short on materials, could not compete in the race to build ironclads, but it did produce some that terrorized the rivers and coastline. The Arkansas damaged the Union fleet at Vicksburg and took part in an attack on Baton Rouge, Louisiana, in August 1863. The Albemarle plied the coast near Plymouth, North Carolina, and briefly paralyzed Union operations there.

Rivets *Smoke stack* *Iron plate*

Entrance hatch *Pointed, ramming bow*

C.S.S. ALBERMARLE
The Albermarle terrorized Union forces along the North Carolina Coast in 1864. She was sunk by a party of Union sailors using a steam-powered launch with a spar torpedo.

C.S.S. ARKANSAS
This armored Confederate ram campaigned in the Vicksburg, Mississippi, area. In August 1862 she headed for battle at Baton Rouge, Louisiana. But her engines broke down near an enemy position, so her crew ran her aground and blew her up.

Confederate naval pennant *Anchor* *Cannon* *Launch* *Davit* *Confederate flag*

CUTLASS AND SCABBARD

This weapon belonged to Confederate Navy Lieutenant W.P.A. Campbell of the ironclad C.S.S. McRae. Even on ironclads, the officers and crew were armed. While the cutlass was a traditional weapon, sailors carried carbines and pistols that were not.

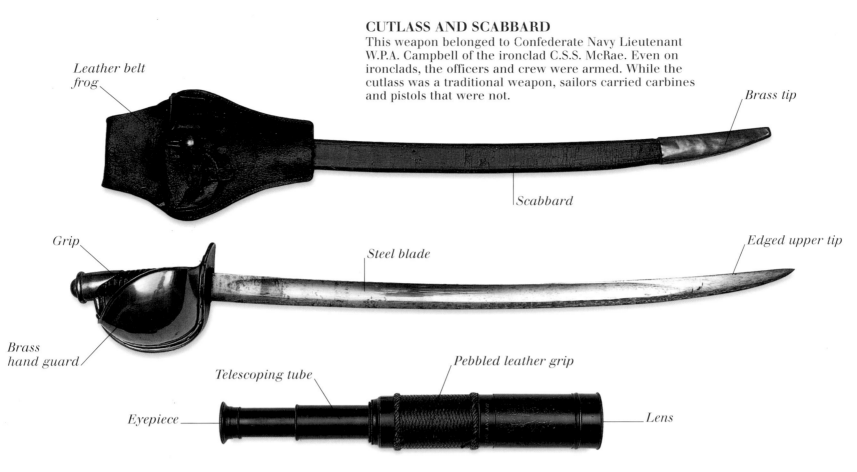

Leather belt frog

Brass tip

Scabbard

Grip

Steel blade

Edged upper tip

Brass hand guard

Telescoping tube

Pebbled leather grip

Eyepiece

Lens

UNION NAVY TELESCOPE

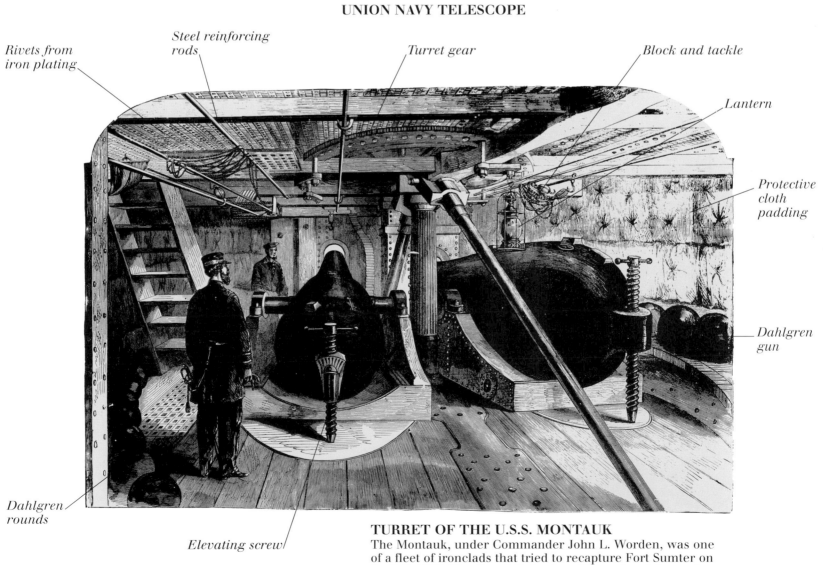

Rivets from iron plating

Steel reinforcing rods

Turret gear

Block and tackle

Lantern

Protective cloth padding

Dahlgren gun

Dahlgren rounds

Elevating screw

TURRET OF THE U.S.S. MONTAUK

The Montauk, under Commander John L. Worden, was one of a fleet of ironclads that tried to recapture Fort Sumter on April 7, 1863. The fleet failed miserably, and took heavy losses.

Photography

PORTRAIT OF A LADY

PHOTOGRAPHY, WHICH WAS developed in the 1830s, had already inspired many avid collectors by the time the war broke out in 1861. Both Northerners and Southerners fully expected to see views of their troops in war. Northern photographers followed the Union armies, making views of soldiers in camp, on campaign, and after battles. They documented gruesome hospital scenes and, for the first time, showed civilians what dead and wounded soldiers looked like lying on the battlefield. Mathew Brady is the most famous of the Northern Civil War photographers, but he actually took few pictures during the conflict. His studio employed "camera operators" who traveled with the armies. Two who took some of the war's most famous photographs were Timothy O'Sullivan and Alexander Gardner. Several Southern photographers had hoped to follow the same course, but the industry-poor Confederacy manufactured few of the chemicals they needed, and the Union navy's blockade of Southern ports drastically restricted the import of photographic materials. Consequently, most Confederate photography was done in studios, where chemicals could be better conserved, and the Confederate photographic record consists almost entirely of formal portraits. Those taken outdoors by Southern camera men are rarities. Studio photographers in the North and South also produced thousands of palm-size portraits called *cartes-de-visite* that soldiers and civilians exchanged with one another.

MATHEW B. BRADY

The name Mathew Brady is the most famous among Northern Civil War photographers. The photographic entrepreneur himself posed for this portrait after coming back in from the field following the Union army rout at the July 1861 Battle of Bull Run in Virginia. Brady had never seen a battle, and did not understand that there would be no opportunities for him to ply his craft amid all the chaos.

Linen photographer's duster

A soldier in the antebellum uniform of a "voltigeur," an elite skirmisher who served in advance of the infantry

Brass hinge

Velvet lining

Embossed leather

CASED PORTRAITS

At the outset of the Civil War, the folks at home displayed portraits of their men in uniform in the parlor. Soldiers in the field carried pictures in lockets or hard cases. Portraits were kept in hinged leather cases to safeguard the expensive photographs inside. Studio operators made their money selling these decorative cases, as well as making the portraits.

Ambrotype image of a little girl

Brass frame

CAMERA

Cameras in the 1860s had no lens shutters. The photographer simply pulled away the lens cap for the number of seconds needed to expose the negative.

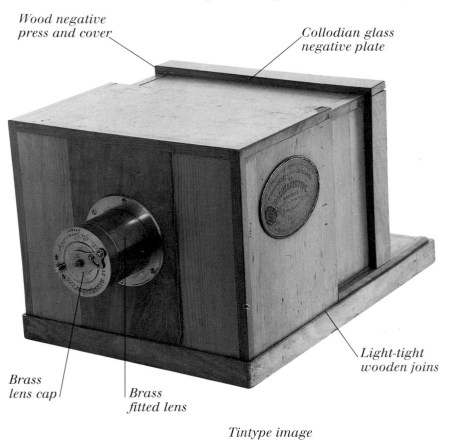

Wood negative press and cover

Collodian glass negative plate

Brass lens cap

Brass fitted lens

Light-tight wooden joins

FUTURE GENERAL EARL VAN DORN

The antebellum fad for photography ensured that images of some famous men would be preserved for posterity. Southern rake Van Dorn had pre-war military experience on the Western frontier. There are not many photographs of him, because he was killed during the war by a jealous husband.

RARE PHOTO OF CONFEDERATES OUTDOORS

This rare outdoor photo is of Dreaux's Battalion of Louisiana troops, photographed at Pensacola, Florida, in May 1861.

Harpers Ferry rifle musket

Custom-made uniforms

Tintype image of a soldier

Handwritten pledge was inserted here

Gold plating

PLEDGE LOCKET

A mother, wife, or sweetheart kept a soldier's portrait in this locket, along with his handwritten pledge to stand by the Confederacy, come what may.

Fob

Brass coin

Unusual weapons

UNION-MADE STEEL BODY ARMOR
Taken from the body of the lieutenant colonel of the 11th Connecticut Volunteer Infantry by Confederate Commodore William Wallace Hunter. This armor could deflect bullets, but it was no protection from a shot to the head.

THE CIVIL WAR DEMONSTRATED the old military adage that every new war begins with the weapons and tactics of the last war. The generals of the Union and Confederacy were West Point-trained men, taught the tactics Napoleon used to conquer Europe. During the Mexican War of the 1840s, nothing about beating the under-prepared Mexican army had changed their Napoleonic approach to combat. Likewise, they went into Civil War battles ordering their troops to fire their single-shot rifles en mass, then to charge the enemy armed only with bayonets – just as Napoleon had directed his soldiers. They never took into account that their enemy's single-shot weapons were more powerful and accurate than those of Napoleon's era. Nor did they consider how much more powerful and accurate their own artillery was. These miscalculations alone accounted for thousands of needless combat deaths. The beginning of the end of the Civil War came in Virginia, around Richmond and Petersburg. Many of the items and tactics the Union and Confederate armies experimented with there, and between 1861 and 1865 – trench warfare, automatic weapons, and aerial observation – pointed the way toward the modern, more destructive form of warfare seen in Europe in 1914.

UNION KETCHUM HAND GRENADE
Confederates in the trenches at Vicksburg would catch thrown Ketchum grenades in blankets and heave them back at the Union soldiers. It would be a few decades before armies developed grenades guaranteed to be lethal.

Stiff paper stabilizing fins

Light wooden stem

Steel grenade jacket; most models were made of iron

If the grenade did not land on its nose, it did not explode

Detonation plunger plate exploded the grenade

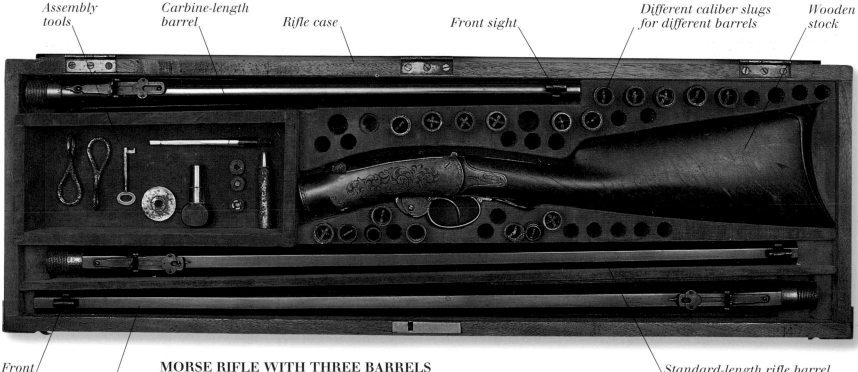

Assembly tools

Carbine-length barrel

Rifle case

Front sight

Different caliber slugs for different barrels

Wooden stock

Front sight

Heavy-caliber hunting barrel

MORSE RIFLE WITH THREE BARRELS
This patent 1856 weapon, one of only 100 made, had interchangeable barrels. It was carried in the Civil War by Confederate John M. Landiga, an officer and former Louisiana politician.

Standard-length rifle barrel

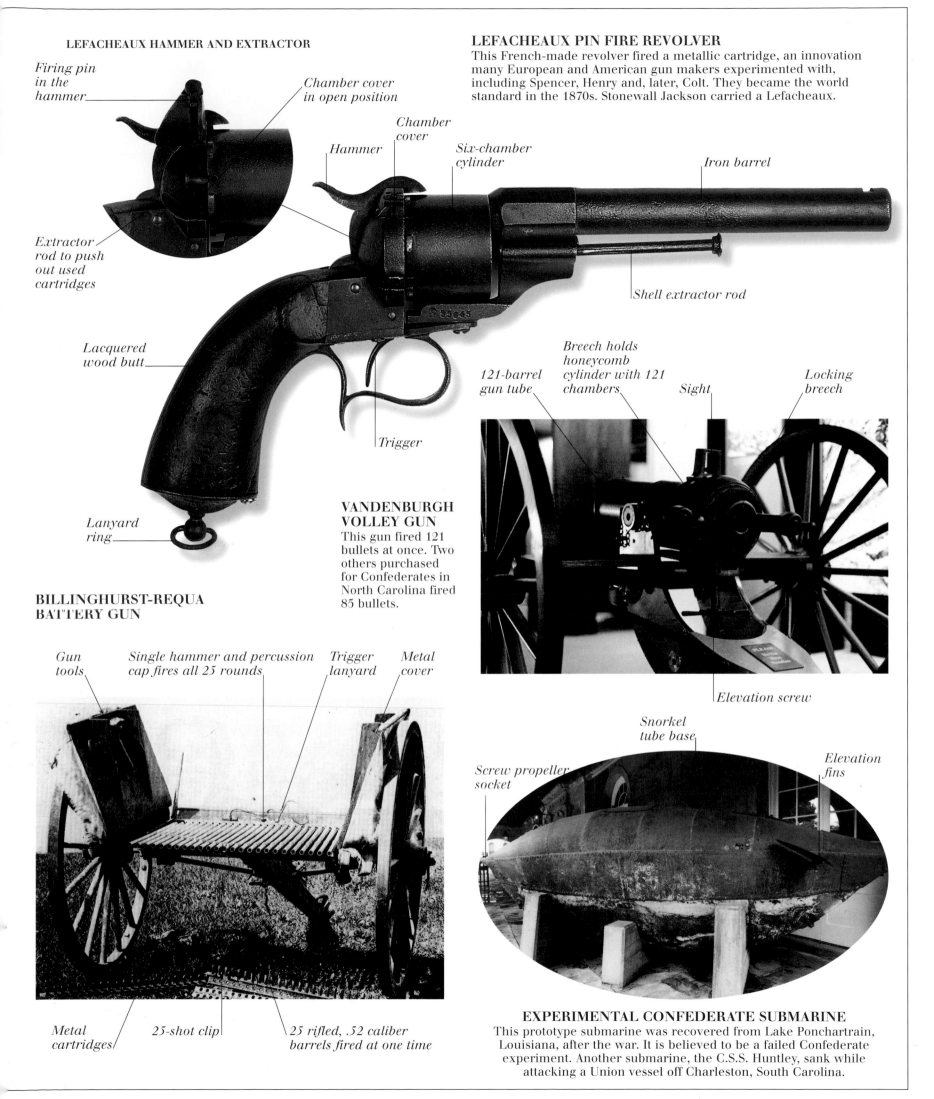

LEFACHEAUX HAMMER AND EXTRACTOR

Firing pin in the hammer

Chamber cover in open position

Extractor rod to push out used cartridges

Lacquered wood butt

Lanyard ring

LEFACHEAUX PIN FIRE REVOLVER
This French-made revolver fired a metallic cartridge, an innovation many European and American gun makers experimented with, including Spencer, Henry and, later, Colt. They became the world standard in the 1870s. Stonewall Jackson carried a Lefacheaux.

Hammer

Chamber cover

Six-chamber cylinder

Iron barrel

Shell extractor rod

Trigger

VANDENBURGH VOLLEY GUN
This gun fired 121 bullets at once. Two others purchased for Confederates in North Carolina fired 85 bullets.

121-barrel gun tube

Breech holds honeycomb cylinder with 121 chambers

Sight

Locking breech

Elevation screw

BILLINGHURST-REQUA BATTERY GUN

Gun tools

Single hammer and percussion cap fires all 25 rounds

Trigger lanyard

Metal cover

Metal cartridges

25-shot clip

25 rifled, .52 caliber barrels fired at one time

Snorkel tube base

Screw propeller socket

Elevation fins

EXPERIMENTAL CONFEDERATE SUBMARINE
This prototype submarine was recovered from Lake Ponchartrain, Louisiana, after the war. It is believed to be a failed Confederate experiment. Another submarine, the C.S.S. Huntley, sank while attacking a Union vessel off Charleston, South Carolina.

Souvenirs and relics

CIVIL WAR SOLDIERS INTENSELY pursued the Victorian passion for collecting. Zealous and odd as this collecting sometimes became, it did guarantee that the Civil War would be the best-documented episode in American history. Soldiers often dismantled historical sites just moments after an event took place. For instance, when Confederate General Robert E. Lee surrendered to Union General Ulysses S. Grant, the table on which Lee signed the surrender document was immediately swept up by Union Major General Philip Sheridan. Sheridan then shipped it to his friend Elizabeth Custer, wife of his subordinate, George Armstrong Custer. This invaluable historic relic became a Custer family heirloom. Sometimes this impulse to gather relics proved disruptive. Following President Abraham Lincoln's assassination at Ford's Theater in Washington, D.C., on April 15, 1865, items were quickly snatched from the theater – some that could have proved important as evidence. Souvenir swatches were even cut from the dead Lincoln's clothing by collectors. Years later, the blood-stained rocker in which Lincoln had been sitting turned up in the personal museum collection of industrialist Henry Ford.

CENTER OF THE BATTLE FLAG OF THE 18TH LOUISIANA INFANTRY
Rather than surrender their flag to the U.S. government at the end of the war, the officers of the 18th tore it into 10 pieces – one for each company commander.

Made from Fort Sumter's shattered flagstaff

SECESSION COCKADE
Worn on lapels or hats in the weeks before the Civil War, these ribbons showed that the wearer supported secession. This one is from Louisiana.

Button with state symbol, in this case a pelican

Pleated ribbon

Originally blue, now black with age

GENERAL BEAUREGARD'S WALKING STICK
P.G.T. Beauregard commanded the forces that bombarded Fort Sumter and forced its surrender. This walking stick was presented to the general as a souvenir of his victory.

SOUVENIR COPY OF LEE'S MESSAGE TO HIS TROOPS ANNOUNCING HIS SURRENDER
General Robert E. Lee surrendered his Army of Northern Virginia in April 1865. Other Confederate troops in the field surrendered by June. Loyal ex-Confederates paid for reprints of Lee's dignified and gentle assessment of their situation and performance.

General Order No. 9

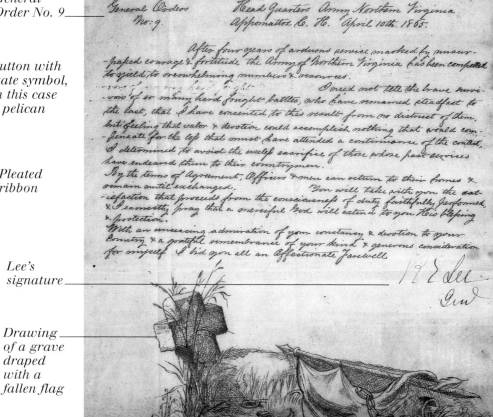

Lee's signature

Drawing of a grave draped with a fallen flag

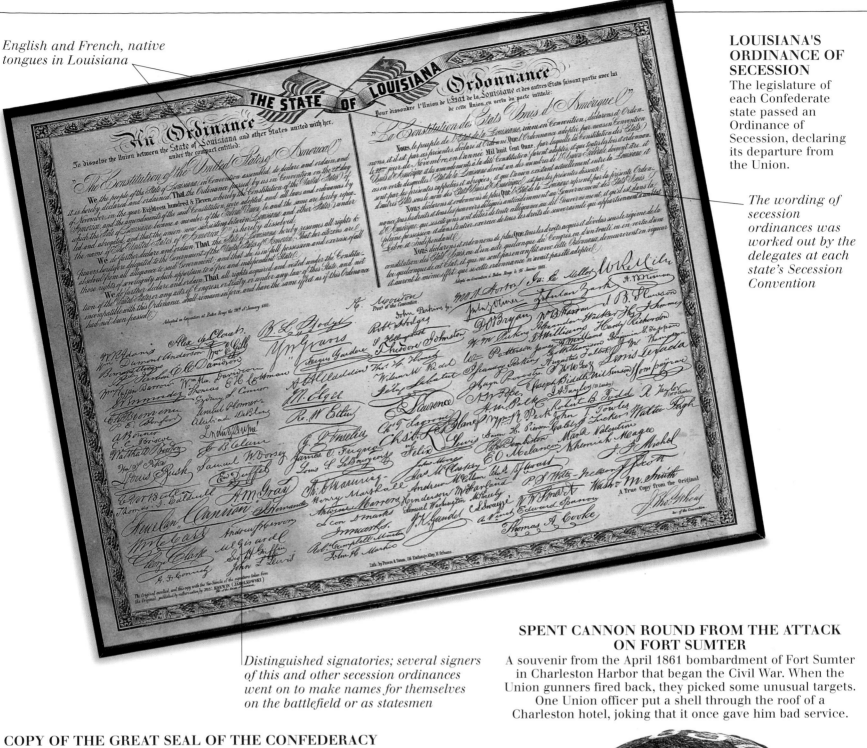

English and French, native tongues in Louisiana

The wording of secession ordinances was worked out by the delegates at each state's Secession Convention

Distinguished signatories; several signers of this and other secession ordinances went on to make names for themselves on the battlefield or as statesmen

SPENT CANNON ROUND FROM THE ATTACK ON FORT SUMTER
A souvenir from the April 1861 bombardment of Fort Sumter in Charleston Harbor that began the Civil War. When the Union gunners fired back, they picked some unusual targets. One Union officer put a shell through the roof of a Charleston hotel, joking that it once gave him bad service.

COPY OF THE GREAT SEAL OF THE CONFEDERACY
The original Great Seal of the Confederate States of America was shipped to Bermuda upon the collapse of the secessionist government. It returned to the South in the 20th century and is now kept at the Museum of the Confederacy in Richmond, Virginia.

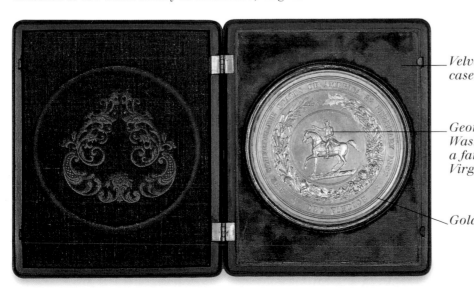

Velvet-lined case

George Washington, a famous Virginian

Gold plate

Cast iron ball

FIRED FROM FORT MOULTRIE INTO CHARLESTON, S.C. 1861

Index

Acknowledgments

Dorling Kindersley would like to thank the following for their kind permission to photograph at their establishments: Gettysburg National Military Park, National Park Service, Department of the Interior; Confederate Memorial Hall, New Orleans, Louisiana; U.S. Army Military History Institute, Carlisle, Pennsylvania.

Picture Credits:
Pages 6-7: Homespun Confederate infantry uniform, Gettysburg National Military Park; wooden canteen, Confederate Memorial Hall; Enfield rifle, Gettysburg National Military Park; Harpers Ferry rifle, Gettysburg National Park; infantryman's cartridge box, Confederate Memorial Hall; infantryman's rifle cap box, Confederate Memorial Hall; steel spike bayonet, Gettysburg National Military Park; Union infantryman's fatigue cap, Confederate Memorial Hall; sword bayonet, Gettysburg National Military Park; photograph of 150th Pennsylvania Volunteers, U.S. Army Military History Institute.
Pages 8-9: Photograph of Union army officers with heavy artillery pieces, National Archives; flag of Company 5 Washington Artillery, Confederate Memorial Hall; Maynard carbine, Confederate Memorial Hall; Boyle, Gamble & MacFee artillery saber, Confederate Memorial Hall; U.S. Army artillery short sword, Gettysburg National Military Park; artilleryman's fuse pouch, Confederate Memorial Hall; Confederate artillery officer's kepi, Confederate Memorial Hall; wheeled field artillery ammunition chest, Gettysburg National Military Park; Union artilleryman's cap insignia, U.S. Army Military History Institute; Major D.C. Merwin's mangled artillery jacket and left hand gloves, Confederate Memorial Hall.
Pages 10-11: Union army cavalryman's uniform, Gettysburg National Military Park; sketch of 1st Virginia Cavalry, Library of Congress; Sharps carbine, Gettysburg National Military Park; Tranter revolver, Confederate Memorial Hall; U.S. Army dragoon pistol-carbine, Gettysburg National Military Park; cavalry boots, Confederate Memorial Hall; cavalry saddle, Confederate Memorial Hall; saddle bags, Confederate Memorial Hall; Confederate cavalry spurs, Confederate Memorial Hall; saber and scabbard of P.P. Brewer, Confederate Memorial Hall.
Pages 12-13: Photograph of Union navy crew, National Archives; Union navy "powder monkey," Library of Congress; painting of C.S.S. Alabama, Confederate Memorial Hall; U.S. Navy cutlass, Gettysburg National Military Park; U.S. Navy pistol and pistol belt, Gettysburg National Military Park; Confederate navy hailing trumpet, Confederate Memorial Hall; U.S. Navy officer's dress chapeau, Gettysburg National Military Park; U.S. Navy officer's dress jacket, Gettysburg National Military Park; pennant of C.S.S. McRae, Confederate Memorial Hall.
Pages 14-15: Cavalry lance, U.S. Army Military History Institute; trooper Charles Masland's lancer jacket, U.S. Army Military History Institute; photograph of Union Zouaves, Corbis Photo Library; Confederate sharpshooter's jacket, Confederate Memorial Hall; sharpshooter's spectacles, collection of Dr. Keith Cangelosi, Confederate Memorial Hall; photograph of Captain Alexander White, Confederate Memorial Hall; mannequin in uniform of Union Zouave, Gettysburg National Military Park; photograph of Colonel Hiram Berdan, U.S. Army Military History Institute.
Pages 16-17: U.S.C.T. recruiting poster, Vermont Historical Association; Lieutenant Montieau's canteen, Confederate Memorial Hall; photograph of 1st Louisiana Native Guard member, collection of Dr. Keith Cangelosi, Confederate Memorial Hall; flag of 2nd U.S.C.T. regiment; Courtesy Commonwealth of Massachusetts, photo by Douglas Christian; lithograph "Come and Join Us Brothers," Library of Congress; U.S. Infantry Tactics manual, U.S. Army Military History Institute; photograph of Confederate half-brother, collection of Dr. Keith Cangelosi, Confederate Memorial Hall; photograph of African-American laborers, Library of Congress.
Pages 18-19: Robert E. Lee portrait, Confederate Memorial Hall; Jefferson Davis portrait, Corbis Photo Library; Nathan Bedford Forrest portrait, Confederate Memorial Hall; Braxton Bragg portrait, Confederate Memorial Hall; Braxton Bragg's uniform coat, Confederate Memorial Hall; Braxton Bragg's dress sword and scabbard, Confederate Memorial Hall; Stonewall Jackson portrait, Confederate Memorial Hall; P.G.T. Beauregard portrait, Confederate Memorial Hall;

General Beauregard's epaulets, Confederate Memorial Hall; General Beauregard's spurs, Confederate Memorial Hall; J.E.B. Stuart portrait, Confederate Memorial Hall.
Pages 20-21: Photograph of Abraham Lincoln, Library of Congress; George B. McClellan portrait, Mayer & Stetfield Lithograph, 1862; photograph of U.S. Grant and staff, National Archives; William T. Sherman portrait, Lafayette College, Pennsylvania; General Sherman's campaign hat, U.S. Army Military History Institute.
Pages 22-23: Holstered Colt revolver, U.S. Army Military History Institute; Derringer pistol, Gettysburg National Military Park; pepperbox pistol, Gettysburg National Military Park; arsenal gang mold, Confederate Memorial Hall; .22 caliber Smith & Wesson revolver, Confederate Memorial Hall; .32 caliber Smith & Wesson revolver, Confederate Memorial Hall; Colt "Army" revolver and loading details, U.S. Army Military History Institute; LeMat revolver, Gettysburg National Military Park; Remington revolver, Gettysburg National Military Park.
Pages 24-25: Iron side knife, Gettysburg National Military Park; Confederate wooden sword scabbard, U.S. Army Military History Institute; infantry officer's combat sword, Gettysburg National Military Park; 1860 pattern infantry officer's combat blade, U.S. Army Military History Institute; Union army cavalry saber, Gettysburg National Military Park; Union army officer's dress sword, scabbard, sword belt and red sash, U.S. Army Military History Institute; musician's sword, U.S. Army Military History Institute; D.W. Adam's presentation sword and scabbard, Confederate Memorial Hall; Major General Kilpatrick's presentation sword, U.S. Army Military History Institute; Bowie knife and scabbard, Confederate Memorial Hall.
Pages 26-27: Springfield-model rifle, Gettysburg National Military Park; Tarpley carbine, Confederate Memorial Hall; Burnside carbine, Confederate Memorial Hall; Joslyn carbine, Confederate Memorial Hall; rifle percussion caps, Confederate Memorial Hall; Enfield rifle bullet mold and tools, Confederate Memorial Hall; gunpowder flask, Confederate Memorial Hall; Hall rifle, Confederate Memorial Hall; Jenks carbine, Confederate Memorial Hall; 12-gauge muzzle-loading shotgun, Confederate Memorial Hall.
Pages 28-29: Williams rapid-fire gun, West Point Museum, West Point, New York; 1857 model "Napoleon" gun-howitzer, Gettysburg National Military Park; Rodman guns, Frank Leslie's Illustrated Newspaper.
Pages 30-31: U.S. Navy shell wrench, Confederate Memorial Hall; artilleryman's thumbstall, Confederate Memorial Hall; binoculars and case of Alfred Mouton, Confederate Memorial Hall; brass pendulum hausse and artillery sight, Confederate Memorial Hall; artillerymen sponging out a gun, Frank Leslie's Illustrated Newspaper; case shot and iron balls, Gettysburg National Military Park; shells for rifled cannons, Gettysburg National Military Park; solid iron shot and wooden sabot, Gettysburg National Military Park; tin canister round and lead slugs, U.S. Army Military History Institute; pewter Bormann artillery fuse and paper time fuse packets, Gettysburg National Military Park; metal artillery fuse plugs, Gettysburg National Military Park; Confederate wooden artillery fuse plug, Gettysburg National Military Park.
Pages 32-33: Photograph of Union officers in camp, U.S. Army Military History Institute; tin camp ware, Confederate Memorial Hall; Union soldier's tin canteen with canvas cover, U.S. Army Military History Institute; Confederate currency , Confederate Memorial Hall; leather haversack, U.S. Army Military History Institute; camp coffee bottle, Confederate Memorial Hall; havelock, Confederate Memorial Hall; homemade Confederate knapsack, Confederate Memorial Hall; canvas haversack, Confederate Memorial Hall.
Pages 34-35: Photograph of Confederate soldiers with blanket rolls, U.S. Army Military History Institute; camp desk, inkwell and pen, Confederate Memorial Hall; playing cards, tobacco, pipe, matches case, Confederate Memorial Hall; copy of Hardee's Tactics, U.S. Army Military History Institute; Dixie's Land sheet music, Confederate Memorial Hall; family photo, collection of Dr. Keith Cangelosi, Confederate Memorial Hall; soldier's sewing kit, Confederate Memorial Hall; Harry Hays' pocket watch, Confederate Memorial Hall; whiskey flask, Confederate Memorial Hall; Union soldier's lap desk, stationary, pen nibs, photograph and patriotic envelope, U.S. Army Military History Institute.
Pages 36-37: Photograph of U.S. Army surgeons at work, U.S. Army Military History Institute; statistical table from Confederate army medical manual, Epitome of Practical Surgery, 1862; Confederate Army medical disability certificate, Confederate Memorial Hall; Union army surgical tools, Gettysburg National Military Park;

Union army medical guide page on removing bullets, A Manual of Minor Surgery, 1863; Union army medical guide page on tourniquet use, A Manual of Minor Surgery, 1863.
Pages 38-39: Photograph of escaped slave, U.S. Army Military History Institute; photograph of plantation slave quarters, Louisiana State Museum; bill of sale for slaves, Louisiana State Museum; hand-forged slave collar, Louisiana State Museum; Virginia dealer's slave pen, U.S. Army Military History Institute; slave auction notice, Louisiana State Museum.
Pages 40-41: Prisoner of war parole papers, Confederate Memorial Hall; photograph of Andersonville survivor, Confederate Memorial Hall; prisoners freed from Camp Ford, Texas, Library of Congress; Elmira, New York prisoner of war camp, Library of Congress; lithograph of the Andersonville prison compound, Confederate Memorial Hall; photograph of Fort Delaware Prison, Fort Delaware Society, Eric Crossan, photographer.
Pages 42-43: Portable telegraph key, DK Picture Library; signal drum, The State Museum of Pennsylvania, Pennsylvania Historical and Museum Commission; photograph of field telegrapher's wagon, Library of Congress; Beardslee telegraph and interior details, U.S. Army Signal Corps; Union troops running field telegraph wire, Library of Congress.
Pages 44-45: Cowan's Mississippi Battery flag, Confederate Memorial Hall; Hilliard's Alabama Legion flag, Confederate Memorial Hall; 25th Louisiana Regiment flag, Confederate Memorial Hall; Ware's Tigers regimental flag, Confederate Memorial Hall; 1st Louisiana Special Battalion flag, Confederate Memorial Hall; 54th Massachusetts Regiment flag, Courtesy Commonwealth of Massachusetts, photo by Douglas Christian; 28th Massachusetts Regiment flag, Courtesy Commonwealth of Massachusetts, photo by Douglas Christian; 48th Pennsylvania Regiment flag, The State Museum of Pennsylvania, Pennsylvania Historical and Museum Commission; 51st Pennsylvania Regiment flag, The State Museum of Pennsylvania, Pennsylvania Historical and Museum Commission.
Pages 46-47: Confederate Railway gun, U.S. Army Military History Institute; Dictator mortar, Library of Congress; armored railroad battery, Frank Leslie's Illustrated Newspaper; locomotive "The General," Big Shanty Museum, Kennesaw, Georgia.
Pages 48-49: Photograph of T.C. Lowe in balloon gondola, National Archives; T.C. Lowe's portable gas generators, U.S. Military History Institute; ascension of Lowe's balloon, painting by Sidney King, Berkeley Plantation, Virginia.
Pages 50-51: Cannonball flattened against the Merrimac, U.S. Army Military History Institute; the Merrimac sinking the U.S.S. Congress, Frank Leslie's Illustrated Newspaper; the battle between the Monitor and the Merrimac, Frank Leslie's Illustrated Newspaper; cross-section of the Monitor's turret, Battles and Leaders of the Civil War; cutaway view of the Monitor, Battles and Leaders of the Civil War.
Pages 52-53: Primitive painting of C.S.S. Tennessee, Confederate Memorial Hall; portrait of C.S.S. Arkansas, Confederate Memorial Hall; photograph of C.S.S. Albemarle, U.S. Naval Historical Center; Confederate navy cutlass and scabbard, Confederate Memorial Hall; U.S. Navy telescope, Confederate Memorial Hall; Turret of U.S.S. Montauk, Frank Leslie's Illustrated Newspaper.
Pages 54-55: Photograph of unidentified lady, U.S. Army Military History Institute; photograph of voltigeur, U.S. Army Military History Institute; portrait of little girl, Confederate Memorial Hall; photographic portrait case, U.S. Army Military History Institute; portrait of Mathew Brady, U.S. Army Military History Institute; Civil War-era camera, DK Picture Library; portrait of Earl Van Dorn, Confederate Memorial Hall; photograph of Dreaux's Battalion, Confederate Memorial Hall; pledge locket, Confederate Memorial Hall.
Pages 56-57: Body armor, Confederate Memorial Hall; cased Morse rifle, Confederate Memorial Hall; steel jacketed Ketchum hand grenade, Gettysburg National Military Park; photograph of LeFacheaux Revolver and hammer detail, Gettysburg National Military Park; Vandenburgh Volley Gun, Petersburg National Battlefield, Petersburg, Virginia; Billinghurst-Requa Battery, National Archives; Confederate submarine, Louisiana State Museum.
Pages 58-59: General Beauregard's walking stick, Confederate Memorial Hall; secession cockade, Confederate Memorial Hall; fragment of 18th Louisiana Regiment flag, Confederate Memorial Hall; souvenir copy of Lee's surrender message, Confederate Memorial Hall; Louisiana's Ordinance of Secession, Confederate Memorial Hall; copy of Great Seal of the Confederacy, Confederate Memorial Hall; cannon ball from 1861 fight